RAF
BRIZE NORTON

Wilf Pereira

Patrick Stephens Limited, a member of the Haynes Publishing Group, has published authoritative, quality books for enthusiasts for a quarter of a century. During that time the company has established a reputation as one of the world's leading publishers of books on aviation, maritime, military, model-making, motor cycling, motor racing, railway and railway modelling subjects. Readers or authors with suggestions for books they would like to see published are invited to write to: The Editorial Director, Patrick Stephens Limited, Sparkford, Nr. Yeovil, Somerset, BA22 7JJ.

RAF
BRIZE NORTON
Gateway to the World

Wilf Pereira

Patrick Stephens Limited

First published 1993

© Wilf Pereira 1993

British Library Cataloguing-in-Publication Data:
A catalogue record for this book is available from the British Library.

ISBN 1-85260-436-0

Library of Congress Catalog card no. 92-75813

Title page: The Station's emergency services practising evacuation procedures on a
VC10 of No. 10 Squadron.

Typeset by BPCC Techset Ltd, Hennock Road, Marsh Barton, Exeter, Devon.

Printed in Great Britain by BPCC Wheatons Ltd, Hennock Road, Marsh Barton,
Exeter, Devon.

Contents

Acknowledgements

Acknowledgements should go first to those RAF Brize Norton personnel who provided every assistance with this book. Brize is a busy place, yet one and all found time to help. Naming each helper would create too long a list, but they should be thanked collectively for their generous contributions.

Some names, however, must be mentioned. Most of the photographs were made available by Sergeant John Readshaw of the Station's Photographic Section. Others were contributed by Flight Refuelling of Wareham, Kev Darling of BBA Photos and Molly White, a local aviation writer. They make a fine selection.

Then there was Wing Commander David Ingham, OC Admin Wing, who made the overall arrangements, and Flight Lieutenant Jim Wilcox CRO, who handled the day-to-day working over many months. No matter when I rang or wrote to Jim he would immediately ensure that all problems were solved and every query answered.

Another person to whom I am grateful is Warrant Officer George Nute in the Engineering Wing. With a little of that 'gentle persuasion' which RAF WOs acquire he made sure the engineering side, particularly that of Brize Norton's Base Hangar, was included and I have him to thank for an interesting chapter.

Last but not least, I should thank two top people at RAF Brize Norton. The first was Wing Commander Dave McDonnell, OC Ops Wing at the time. Instinctively he seemed to know when I wanted information and simply supplied it. The other was Group Captain Keith Filbey, Station Commander, who trusted me on his patch.

Chapter 1

MORNING DEPARTURE

RAF Brize Norton in Oxfordshire is such a large, diverse and complex place that it is difficult for a newcomer to learn, let alone understand, its many ramifications. Even those who have been there for many months, concentrating on particular duties, admit they have insufficient knowledge of the rest. The powers that be endeavour to keep everyone informed, but so much is going on all the time. As for outsiders, they tend to know about just one or two activities. To them it is the Station which flies Service people overseas — or it is the venue looking after VIPs. Some will be interested in the VC10s and TriStars, others in air-to-air refuelling. The name Brize Norton is also linked with the Parachute School, the RAF Falcons Team, and with the Falklands and the Gulf Wars.

The purpose of this book is to try to explain some of RAF Brize Norton's multiple activities. To achieve this it is first necessary to separate the various parts of Station life and look at them individually.

The place is popularly called 'Gateway to the World'. Service men and women, their families, civil servants, ministers and royalty have all gone through its portals. There is a gateway in the Station badge, and the motto 'Transire Confidenter' freely translates to 'Pass through Confidently'. There is also a Station hotel named Gateway House and a monthly magazine called *Gateway*.

Chapter 1 will deal with the transportation aspect. RAF Brize Norton's Gateway remains open 24 hours a day, every day, and handles 180,000 air passengers a year. The Station gets them away and brings them back again with the maximum of efficiency and the minimum of fuss. Behind-the-scenes details of how it is done will come later, but first let us follow a typical Service passenger posted overseas.

The typical Service passenger could be a young RAF Sergeant in the Administrative Branch. He has been posted to Washington DC for two years and will be accompanied by his wife together with their two small children. A wife and family is included in this story because the situation is not uncommon and it also exemplifies the overall care provided by the RAF. The Sergeant and his family will travel in civilian clothes and most likely will take an afternoon train from London to Swindon. Other passengers on the train could well be Service personnel — engineers on their way to US Air Force bases in the American Mid-West, parachutists to southern California, a contingent of Royal Marines for jungle warfare training in Belize.

All these Service travellers have had prior instructions on how they will be met and transported. Lists are quickly consulted, identifications checked. Special attention is given to mothers and their children. The group is guided towards the waiting buses for Brize Norton. As soon as the first bus is full, it sets off through the town and into the country. The Admin Sergeant had been Stationed in East Anglia where there was plenty of country, but this part of England is quite different.

Gateway House at RAF Brize Norton, well known to thousands of Service air travellers.

Below right Arrival of Service personnel at Brize Norton Passenger Terminal.

Below The departure lounge incorporates most airport facilities.

Everywhere he looks there is butter-coloured stone. Endless walls are made of it, as are grand manor houses and humble cottages, large farms and even larger barns. He correctly judges these are the Cotswolds, a landscape he had heard about though had never seen.

During the 45-minute journey the buses pass through several villages where every building is made of the same buttery stone. There are signposts pointing to hamlets with quaint names like Broughton Poggs and Filkins. This essentially rural scene is suddenly disturbed by a jet aircraft flying over the bus and climbing away from an as yet invisible airfield. The driver remarks that it is a plane from Brize Norton on its way to the eastern Mediterranean.

An approach sign announces Carterton, the Oxfordshire town that is part and parcel of the air base. There are many shops, three garages, a good library and the

Service personnel check in at Passenger Terminal Reception.

market is on Thursday when farm produce is brought in from the surrounding countryside. After crossing the town centre, RAF Brize Norton makes its presence felt. First sightings include what looks like, and is, a big hotel, an even bigger hangar beyond it and avenues stretching into the far distance between plenty of trees. The attractive lawns and flower beds are, however, accompanied by high fences and armed guards. The buses stop at the main gate for a second check on identities. Only when the Guard Commander is satisfied does each vehicle enter the Station and proceed to its Passenger Terminal.

The terminal building at Brize Norton has the look of Heathrow or Gatwick, though on a smaller, friendlier, more human scale. Luggage is unloaded as the last Service passengers leave the coach. They are helped — and help each other — to stack their bags on trolleys, and they then move into the reception hall. This area has

Far left Check-in follows standard international procedure.

Left RAF Brize Norton's check-in is fully computerized.

9

Below The lounge area in
Gateway House.

smart red-and-white decor, and there is every convenience, including washrooms and dispenser machines for refreshments. As soon as they are ready, passengers check in their bags. There are no long waits. After checking in and receiving their boarding cards, the following morning's passengers will proceed to Gateway House. There, rooms have been reserved for everyone, Service personnel and families alike.

The reception hall at Brize Air Terminal has multiple luggage weighing Stations and a computerized booking system similar to that used by British Airways. In fact, the airline and Brize Norton have many other close links, as will be described later. Meanwhile the names and details of the latest passengers are entered, as are the weights and numbers of bags. Forty-four pounds per person is the norm, with margins built into the system for types of postings and duration of overseas service. Brize has been — in computer parlance — 'number crunching' for many years, so the whole process is relaxed yet brisk. Soon the first passengers are back in their bus and heading for Gateway House.

This transit hotel is surrounded by well-kept lawns, its light brown brickwork looking good as it rises from the green expanse. There are four levels — ground, first, second and third — and also what appears to be a ground floor extension from the higher building. First-time visitors to Gateway House often wonder why the two structures are connected by an overhead bridge. They soon learn that there is more to Gateway House than meets the eye. A great many practical considerations went into its design and fabrication.

The bus stops between the two buildings under the bridging section, a welcome feature to passengers if the weather is unkind. The main entrance into Gateway House is through the single floor unit and the first impression is of a tastefully decorated modern hotel. Its foyer is spacious, with an airy courtyard beyond a broad staircase. There are gleaming floors, leather chesterfields and well-kept indoor plants. Other features include a shop selling a range of books, papers, gifts and confectionery. Children are attracted towards a large lighted fish tank.

The reception desk is to the right of the entrance. Leaving his wife to look after the children, the Admin Sergeant goes to it. The simple standard procedure is to hand over boarding cards in return for room keys. Next morning the procedure will be

Below right Security
checks apply to Service
and civilian passengers
passing through RAF Brize
Norton.

reversed. The Sergeant is informed that he and his family have been allocated two adjoining rooms on the first floor. These are generally given to those with children so that parents do not have to take them up and down too many levels. He is also told that there is a connecting door and two single beds in each room.

As the Sergeant leads his family up the staircase, he begins to understand a little more of the design philosophy which went into the making of Gateway House. The bridge arrangement between the two structures ensures that the reception and social area is kept separate from the sleeping accommodation. Gateway contains 170 twin-bedded rooms in its four-floor block. Everything is built, decorated and furnished to what could be described as 'basic comfort' ideal for overnight stops.

Each door off the carpeted passages opens into a room between two single-size wall beds. Each bed is freshly made up with a pair of clean sheets, blankets sufficient for the season and two plump pillows. There is a wash basin with a light above the back mirror and an electric shaver point next to the light. A generous window gives panoramic views either of the Cotswold countryside or of Brize Norton airfield, depending on the room position. Showers, baths and toilets are just across the passage from the bedroom door. All are spotlessly clean. The VIP rooms are also on the first floor. They consist of three en suite bedrooms and a small dining room for six.

The accommodation block is looked after by a staff of one chief stewardess and ten chambermaids. They change all used bedding every morning. A busy week at Gateway House will mean dealing with between three and four thousand sheets plus pillow slips. These go down a chute from all storeys to a ground floor room from which they are sent out for laundering locally.

While his wife is seeing to the children, the Admin Sergeant retraces his steps to see more of Gateway House. This time he notices there are rooms off the bridge corridor. One is fitted up as a television room with armchairs and a large settee. Another is a games room for children. Further on, a flight of stairs leads up to a viewing area on the roof. From there the Sergeant can see much more of the Station and airfield. To his right is the Passenger Terminal, which he recognizes, with the tailplanes of VC10s and TriStars protruding above other buildings. To his left looms a huge hangar that dominates that side of the air base.

Gateway House bedrooms are functional and comfortable.

This is Base Hangar, the largest building at RAF Brize Norton. It is 1045 ft long by 215 ft wide, thereby covering 5½ acres. The doors on the side facing the airfield can be opened along the entire length and six VC10 aircraft housed within for overhauls. The 90 ft high roof is supported by a system of cantilever frames which give a working height of 50 ft — ample to take the 40 ft high VC10 tailplanes. Work in Base Hangar is carried out by teams of Service and civilian personnel. As well as being told the dimensions of this building, visitors to Brize are given some amusing additional statistics. In one year, hangar personnel consume 10,400 cups of tea or coffee, 15,000 doughnuts and 22,800 bread rolls.

Continuing his exploration of Gateway House, the Sergeant descends to the reception area. More people are arriving for tomorrow morning's departure to Dulles International Airport, Washington DC. He threads his way through them to look at the three sets of lounges, each with a bar, for Junior Ranks, senior NCOs and commissioned officers. All are built and furnished to the same high standard of comfort and exist side by side. The same staff behind the three bars serve everyone. The Junior Ranks Lounge is the largest and has a well-equipped games room integral to it. Beyond is the first bar providing a wide range of drinks and displaying a vast collection of stickers. Called 'zaps', they come from all over the world, being donated by aircrews and passengers. Apart from being a Brize tradition, they demonstrate the valuable contacts the Station enjoys with military air forces and civil airlines. The zaps extend to the other bars, and it continually tests the ingenuity of the staff to find space for them.

There is a large television set in each lounge. Gateway House receives all channels and, in addition, has an extensive video libary. To avoid any hassle, every set and programme is controlled from an office beside Reception. Thus the children can watch cartoons, and Junior Ranks, senior NCOs and officers various thrillers, comedies, westerns or science fiction. It is a system that works very well.

The Admin Sergeant is interested in such details. He talks to the Gateway House staff, and they are pleased to answer his questions. He is asked if he would like to go behind the scenes, for there is yet more to this Establishment than at first meets the eye. A passage from the central bar leads to storerooms and an area for packing that is half full of trolleys. The Sergeant recognizes the trolleys as those used for in-flight drinks. He is informed that two trolleys will be going on the Washington flight, one

outward and the other back.

The Corporal in charge shows him how each trolley is packed. There are four drawers on each side. They contain cans of Coke and lager, and miniature bottles of gin, whisky, rum, vodka and brandy, together with red and white wines. Soft drinks, like orange and lemon squash are free, while the others are chargeable. Profits go into Gateway funds towards new television sets, video films and children's toys. Like any other hotel, there is always something required somewhere.

The Sergeant and his Gateway guide move on to the large all-ranks restaurant, with the much smaller officers' dining room off it. The far wall of the restaurant has floor-to-ceiling windows. Outside is a play area for children with swings, roundabouts and climbing frames set out on the grass. The area is so designed that parents can keep an eye on their offspring, also the playground is carefully enclosed to prevent kids wandering off elsewhere.

A Catering Officer talks about Gateway meals. With economies of manpower and equipment always in mind, and to be able to provide meals at short notice, all meals are on a self-service basis with hot main courses pre-portioned in disposable trays. Starters and sweets are freshly prepared. Most passengers either stay overnight for morning flights or arrive in the morning for afternoon departures. The meals system is therefore designed to meet the needs of these key periods, though provision can be made for any sudden influx — as often happens at RAF Brize Norton.

To all authorized passengers breakfast is available within 15 minutes of a call, be it three or four in the morning. Lunches are normally for those held up due to various circumstances, and bookings for these are made after breakfast. Gateway House, the catering officer explains, is more of an evening and night place. Early evening meal times for children are available by pre-arrangement through Reception.

Through the kitchen lies a different and yet more interesting part of the Gateway complex — that concerned with in-flight catering. A staff of 50 (40 Service and 10 civilians) maintains this operation every hour of every day throughout the year. Unsolicited letters of praise are regularly received and the catering officer picks up the latest from his in-tray. It reads:

This is a short note to express my feelings on the standard of meals produced by Brize for flight catering. Compared with almost all other places we visit, the meals from Brize are of a more consistently high standard than from anywhere else. Your efforts are much appreciated and I should like to say thank you to all involved. Please keep it up.

The letter is signed by a Squadron Leader.

Logically, the preparation of in-flight meals is geared to aircraft movements. This procedure involves detailed knowledge of route diaries, flight plans, departure times and passenger lists. Put another way, the in-flight catering staff need to know what sort of aircraft, where to and when — at the earliest possible stage. Short-notice flights apart, preparations usually begin three full days before take-off. A start is made by assembling such items as cups, saucers, plates, knives, forks and spoons, paper napkins, and those countless little capsules containing various condiments.

The Flight Catering Form, from which everyone works, is a formidable double-sided document. It starts by identifying the aircraft, aircrew, passenger total and flight plan. It then lists such tasty-sounding items as nuts, crisps, choc bars and club sandwiches. These are only the snacks. The main courses are much more mouth-watering. Beginning with a choice of breakfasts — English, Continental and Vegetarian — the list goes on to the lunch and dinner-time dishes like Chicken Chasseur, Beef Madeira, Veal Blanquette or Rainbow Trout. After that there are sweets such as trifles, fruit salads, pastries and cakes. Main courses come from specialist in-flight caterers at Heathrow, as served by the world's best airlines, while Brize sees to the starters and sweets as previously mentioned.

The in-flight catering staff at Brize produces a yearly average of 30,000 crew meals and 160,000 passenger meals. The storage and preparation of food is carried out under strict hygienic conditions. There are three walk-in freezers. Whenever necessary, prepared foods such as salads and sandwiches are wrapped and sealed to keep them fresh. There is one storeroom gleaming with VIP cutlery and crockery — plain, crested and Royal. The Royal porcelain is pure white and gold rimmed.

At this point in the Sergeant's tour the Service children in and around Gateway House are ready for their tea. This is an informal affair of biscuits and cakes, jams and jellies, high chairs and non-spill plastic cups. Staff members cheerfully help parents. It is a fine evening and afterwards many of the infants play outside. Others head for the games room. Gateway personnel have, through training and experience, acquired the valuable gift of keeping control while not appearing to do so.

Dinner is equally informal. Individuals, couples and groups arrive, select their meals and tables, then indulge in Service small talk that is both sociable and valuable in their chosen careers. What happened to so-and-so? Did he or she get promoted? What are the latest deployments, postings, reorganizations? The Admin Sergeant is pleased when a secretary at the British Embassy in Washington — to which he has been posted — asks to share their table. She offers to show them round Washington, listing and commenting on some of the sights — the White House (small), Capitol Hill (impressive), the Smithsonian Museum (inspiring) and Arlington Cemetery (moving).

The secretary congratulates the Sergeant on his prestigious posting (do well, and who knows?) and also offers to take his wife shopping (in what they call malls).

After dinner and checking on the children, the Sergeant and his wife ring their respective parents. A Royal Marines Sergeant is in the next call booth. He waits and, when they emerge, invites them for a drink. The Marines Sergeant says that he and the others are on their way to jungle exercises in Belize. He is an old tropical hand but, while his men are keen, they are in for a surprise. He likes watching their faces when they step out of the plane and into a hundred degrees of heat. The Marine talks knowledgeably about the ancient Central American civilizations, before switching to the Gulf War. Yes, he was there in southern, and later northern, Iraq.

Travellers retire early at Gateway House. By eleven all is silent, especially in the accommodation block. The passengers were told the exact times of their morning calls when they booked in at Reception. They wake, listen to what the receptionist says, then press their white acknowledgement buttons. On vacating their rooms after breakfast they take their overnight luggage with them. When they hand the room keys in at Reception they get back their boarding cards.

Transport from Gateway House to the Passenger Terminal is ready and waiting. An RAF VC10 with its Service and civilian passengers leaves Brize Norton for Washington three mornings a week — on Mondays, Wednesdays and Fridays. Several Ministry of Defence and other government officials will be joining the flight. Their drivers report by car phones that they are well past Oxford and approaching Brize Norton.

Arrangements at the Passenger Terminal are much the same as at an international airport. Indeed RAF Brize Norton deals with a wider range and greater variety of operations than most airfields. Similarly, while passenger and baggage handling compare with that at Heathrow and Gatwick, the process is more friendly and direct. For this flight to Dulles the VC10 is parked right outside the departure lounge. As passengers begin to move through the terminal towards it they are attended by Air Movements staff, ensuring that identities, passports and boarding cards coincide.

Once these precautionary measures are over, the passengers assemble in the departure lounge. There they receive a briefing on the now imminent flight — weather conditions, possible diversions, any special circumstances. On Service flights, a Passenger Reporting Officer is appointed. He is usually a senior commissioned officer and briefed at check-in. This officer must — for his sins — mix with the rest of

Brize Norton's VIP lounge provides a due means of privacy rather than undue luxury.

his fellow passengers, obtain their views about the flight and make a report at the end of it. If there are problems, he has to deal with them on the spot, whilst any complaints have to be recorded. It is called feedback.

There are three VIP levels regularly handled by Air Movements at RAF Brize Norton. The first goes up to the ranks of Air Commodore and Air Vice Marshal. These check in like everyone else, then they are taken to the VIP lounge and looked after by the Duty Air Movements Officer. The second level is for Air Marshals upwards, their equivalent other service ranks and government ministers. These have a police escort, drive straight into the Station through a swift-entry gate and are taken to a side door of the terminal which leads again into the VIP lounge. The third VIP level is the top. His or Her limousine, duly escorted and saluted, will draw up by the front door of the VIP lounge where the Station Commander, no less, is waiting to do the honours.

VIP visitors to RAF Brize Norton. (Left to right) Wing Commander D. McDonnell welcoming visitors Marshal of the Royal Air Force, The Lord Elworthy and Air Vice Marshal Adamson, Chief of the RNZAF Air Staff.

A Brize Norton VC10 at RAF Akrotiri, Cyprus.

However, neither rank nor service is allowed to complicate boarding the aircraft. Compared with certain civil airline practices, the Brize Norton procedure is simple and precise. Passengers leave the departure lounge in seating sequence. A short walk takes them to the plane steps. The Loadmaster, who has been working for some hours to ensure correct loading, seating and catering, performs yet another check — a final head count — as people pass. The VIPs, if there are any on the flight, board last. Once aboard, settling down and belting in proceeds as on civil aircraft.

There are, however, two main differences when flying in an RAF VC10 passenger plane as compared to current civil airline practice. The VC10 has a flight deck crew of four — captain, co-pilot, navigator and air engineer — instead of the more usual civil crew of two or perhaps three. With the RAF TriStar, the four man crew is reduced to three because that aircraft is fitted with an automatic navigation system. The second and very noticeable difference on the VC10 is that all the passenger seats

Brize Norton TriStars at Mount Pleasant airfield, the Falkland Islands.

16

face rearwards. They were designed that way at the time as an additional safety measure for Service personnel. The TriStar seats are stressed to face forwards.

Departure of a VC10 flight from Brize Norton to Dulles International Airport, Washington.

While the VC10 bound for Dulles is preparing to leave, a TriStar comes in to land. It taxies towards the terminal building and nods to a stop. Its passengers have arrived from the Falklands. Apart from RAF and Army personnel, they include what are called 'indulgence passengers' (those who pay for spare seats) and foreign nationals. Surprisingly these include Russian and Korean fishermen returning home by the quickest route from the fish-rich waters of the South Atlantic and Antarctica. The newcomers walk in ones and twos straight into Brize's arrival hall. The hold of the TriStar is already open and luggage is being swiftly transferred to the collection area. Immigration and Customs and Excise formalities will follow.

The VC10's four Conway engines are installed in pairs on each side of the tailplane. This arrangement makes them very quiet for crew and passengers, especially

Arrival of a TriStar flight from the Falklands to RAF Brize Norton.

Service air transport (old style). No.216 Squadron moves the Northamptonshire Regiment in a Vickers Vimy.

in flight. The cabin barely quivers when they are run up, and preliminary movement of the aircraft, as it taxies past the TriStar, is equally smooth. Even at take-off the noise level remains low for those inside the aircraft, though the rest of the Station knows about it.

A light wind prevails from the south-west and the aircraft lifts off in that direction. The neatly patterned fields and woods suddenly sink, diminish and disappear. To the Sergeant and his family, it is a new phase in their lives. To RAF Brize Norton, it is another air movement.

Service transport (new style). Return of Servicemen from the Falklands.

Chapter 2

COTSWOLD AIRBASE

Within an hour's drive from London, shortly after by-passing Oxford's dreaming spires, the Cotswolds begin. The climb from eastward is imperceptible because the whole area resembles a tilted tabletop. About 30 miles westward, Cleeve Cloud overlooks the Severn Valley and a rock-edged escarpment curves 30 miles further to Bristol.

It could be claimed that English genius for improvisation is alive and well at RAF Brize Norton. Descendants of those who lived and worked in the Cotswolds merely turned their inherent skills to creating, adapting and operating — for over half a century — what is now the RAF's biggest and busiest air base.

The period has been an incredible one. It started with the uneasy peace of the 1930s and erupted into the 1939-45 World War that was in turn prolonged by a Cold War. It was also a period of tremendous aeronautical change, occurring alongside a series of international disasters, the most recent being yet another war — this time in the Gulf.

The following paragraphs and selection of old photographs are intended to show the background to Brize Norton rather than provide a definitive history. Most of this book is about contemporary activities, and these can best be appreciated by mentioning the key events leading up to them. How did Brize begin? What took place before the scene which greets present-day visitors?

During the 1930s and the steadily increasing menace of the Third Reich, Britain seemed to be asleep. However, much was going on below the surface, particularly in the Royal Air Force, and Brize Norton formed part of its expansion programme. The area was surveyed, and eventually a site was chosen between the village of Brize Norton and Carterton. Interestingly, the latter was to be the Station's name, but this was changed to avoid possible confusion with RAF Cardington.

The initial airfield, laid out in 1935, was almost circular with a grass take-off/landing run of 1000 yards. There were five main hangars to the north-west and four more dispersed ones at various points round the perimeter. As has been known in the Services, accommodation for personnel lagged behind the rest.

Nevertheless, on 13 August 1937, RAF Brize Norton was officially opened and on 7 September the first flying Unit arrived. This was No.2 Flying Training School bringing with it a present day collector's dream of Audax, Fury and Hart aircraft. Regarding that accommodation problem, the records state 'the best was made of temporary wooden huts'!

The RAF was then on an early learning curve. During one training flight from Brize to Wales in bad weather, an entire formation was lost. Another machine came down off the Dorset coast. Two more crashed while on local circuits and bumps. Fortunately, steady progress overcame these trials and tribulations.

A Hawker Hart at No.2 Flying Training School, Brize Norton.

On 10 October 1938, another set of RAF occupants came to Brize Norton. This was one of those ubiquitous maintenance Units — No.6 MU, in fact — without which the Air Force would have ceased to function. Again, the aircraft they kept ready in their hangars and at dispersal sites would brighten the eyes of present-day aviation museum curators. There were Battles, Gladiators and Swordfish, also two Saunders Roe Cloud amphibians. By February 1939, No.6 MU had more than 200 such aircraft.

In May of that fateful year leading up to war, RAF Brize Norton held what would be the last Empire Air Day. The occasion was very different from modern air displays, when the public walks round static aircraft in the morning, then watches them perform in the afternoon. Instead, viewers lined the road along the western side of Brize to see the School's latest monoplane Harvards and Oxfords which were replacing the old biplanes.

The onset of war in September 1939 brought feverish activity to Brize Norton, as

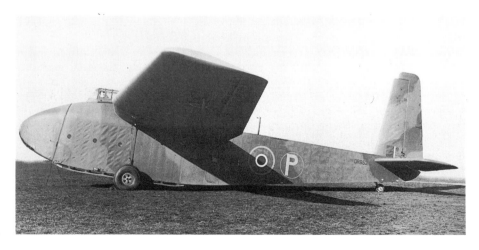

A Hamilcar glider.

elsewhere in the RAF. Aircraft, buildings, and the entire airfield had to be camouflaged. No.2 FlyingTraining School became No.2 Service Flying Training School with many more pupils. Operational Squadrons on scatter exercises came and went.

During the early war months of 1940, No.2 SFTS continued to train and No.6 MU to maintain. France fell, but life at Brize Norton continued to be 99% routine. Suddenly came the 1% action — two JU88s appeared over the Cotswolds and headed straight for the main hangar complex. One hangar, packed full of Oxfords, received a direct hit and the aircraft inside were destroyed. In total, 35 Oxfords and 11 Hurricanes were lost.

Throughout the remainder of 1940 and most of 1941 the pattern continued — training and maintenance, accidents and alarms. By then the airfield had spread into the surrounding countryside, using woods and every other kind of cover for aircraft dispersal. Small hangars suitable for two or three fighters were erected, and it became a common sight to see Hurricanes and Spitfires either being towed or actually taxiing along country lanes.

In 1942, life at RAF Brize Norton entered a very different phase. On 15 July, the Heavy Glider Operational Unit was formed and the Station assumed a front-line role. The RAF was going to train the Army to fly giant gliders. The initial complement consisted of 56 Airspeed Horsa gliders and 34 Armstrong Whitworth Whitley tugs.

Life at Brize — as would often happen in the future — became hectic. Apart from the flying training with all its thrills and spills, No.6 MU was assembling Horsas received direct from factories, also handling American aircraft in the form of Fortresses, Hudsons, Liberators and Mitchells.

Early in 1943, Albemarles began arriving to replace the Whitleys and, within a year, Brize became the base for two Squadrons of these aircraft in glider-tug and paradrop roles. Thus began the Station's association with the art of parachuting that has continued to the present day at No.1 Parachute Training School.

On D-Day, 6 June 1944, Nos.296 and 297 Squadrons from RAF Brize Norton dropped the main body of the 5th Parachute Brigade on Normandy. The job of the first wave was to prepare landing zones for the second, and so it went on throughout that momentous day.

Brize Norton's long association with glider training came to an end on the last day of 1945 when No.21 HGOU moved, taking its Albemarles and Horsas, Halifaxes and Hadrians with it. A lot of old gliders remaining at Brize were sold at knockdown prices for their materials. Many became garden sheds. As for old aircraft, all useful parts were salvaged, and what was left buried in 20 ft deep pits.

The outbreak of peace, as cynics called it, brought no diminution of activities at

A WACO glider.

Right A Horsa glider.

Below Horsa gliders at Brize Norton preparing for D-Day.

A Whitley flies over Horsa gliders.

RAF Brize Norton. The Station was handed over to Transport Command, and a multiplicity of aircraft types were soon seen over the Cotswolds. They included Dakotas, Halifaxes, Liberators, Stirlings and Yorks. It is recorded that one York failed to become airborne, lost its tail while crossing a railway line, but came safely to rest in a nearby field.

From 1945-50 the situation at RAF Brize Norton was one of settling down and experimentation. Air transport, the carrying of Service passengers and equipment, still had to be proven. This was largely done by warplanes with plenty of life left in them, while a new generation of aircraft slowly left the drawing boards.

So the RAF at Brize practised with the aircraft at their disposal, moving increasing quantities of personnel, loading army vehicles, unloading anti-aircraft guns. While this was taking place an American Skymaster crossed the Atlantic and landed without any of its mixed USAF and RAF crew touching the controls. Instead they used a system of radio beams. It showed the shape of things to come.

Dominating that period was the monolithic menace of the Soviet Union, a threat all too clear at the time. At Brize, RAF emphasis was switched, first from Transport to Flying Training, then to Bomber Command. The last was a significant step in the life of the Station. The entire base on the Cotswolds was handed over to the United States Air Force, and they remained there for the next 15 years.

An interesting aspect was the tight and successful security at the time. When a nearby district council began discussing the possibility of American warplanes coming to Brize, a statement from the Air Ministry emphasized that this was not the case.

Above left A Horsa glider, airborne.

Above An Albemarle towing Horsa gliders.

The last flying Lancaster visits Brize Norton for a No.5 Group Reunion.

A Convair B-36, alternatively known as the Peacemaker or an aluminium overcast. *(Courtesy of the Smithsonian Museum)*

Five days later the first Americans arrived.

Even before then, there had been a trickle of specialist personnel arriving at Brize — American Army engineers, airfield surveyors, runway constructors. On 26 August 1950 an engineering battalion began work in earnest, and on 16 April 1951 the Station was officially handed over to the US Air Force.

Major reconstruction, particularly on a much extended and far stronger runway, continued for another year. It was not until June 1952 that people living on the Cotswolds saw and heard the reason why. The misty sky began to throb with the sounds of many, very heavy aircraft. These were 21 Convair B-36 bombers, each with ten engines, known then as Peacemakers. One by one they landed and stayed for a week before flying back to the United States.

A Boeing B-50. Squadrons of these USAF bombers came to Brize Norton for 90-day tours. *(Courtesy of the Smithsonian Museum)*

A Boeing B-47 Stratojet. Hundreds of these maintained a state of instant response at Brize Norton during the Cold War. *(Courtesy of the Smithsonian Museum)*

The next USAF aircraft at Brize were B-50 bombers with KB-29P tankers. Squadrons of these came for 90 days at a time. It was a display of effortless might. It also required extra facilities at Brize, such as a direct fuel line into the base and a new control tower completed on 30 June and 30 August 1953 respectively.

The most important event of that year was the first Boeing B-47 Stratojet Squadron to touch down at Brize. Each Unit came for three months, and hundreds were to maintain a state of instant response to any Soviet threat over the next 12 years.

The United States Air Force operated and maintained the base to high professional standards. Their chief concerns were with the runway and taxiways, as huge jet bombers — B47s and 52s — were the order of the day. The first of the latter arrived on 17 January 1957 having flown direct from a USAF base in California. In later

A Boeing B-52 Stratofortress. The first of its kind arrived at Brize Norton on 17 January 1957 having flown direct from California. *(Courtesy of the Smithsonian Museum)*

Boeing KC-97 Tankers.
Note the flying boom air
refuelling method used by
the US Air Force.
(Courtesy of the
Smithsonian Museum)

years, Brize would have 90 visits by B-52s.

However, the main US aircraft of the period to use Brize were B-47 bombers with KC-97 tankers. Squadrons of them came and went in relentless rotation. The year 1958 began with two B-47 wings — the USAF 68th and 100th — occupying Brize throughout January. One aircraft accidentally jettisoned an underwing fuel tank, which reminded a retired RAF wing commander of his Service days by falling into his back garden.

The United States Air Force, working closely with the Royal Air Force, kept the aerial sword well honed by constant practice, exercises and competitions. Steady advances were also made in aircraft performance to establish new records. For example, in June 1958 two KC-135s flew from New York to Brize in just over five hours. The world was shrinking.

But not Brize Norton. In 1959 a 10,000 ft long runway was completed. Around this time the US Air Force changed to a new pattern of operations called Reflex Action. At Brize this meant halving the B-47s stationed there from 40 to 20 aircraft. In practice the B-47 Units stayed for only three weeks instead of three months with little local flying between their arrivals and departures.

The year 1962 influenced Brize Norton in three very different ways. First it saw the arrival of the Boeing KC-135 tankers which gradually replaced the KC-97s. Second, the Cuban Crisis resulted in a period of instant response alertness. Third, from December onwards, the hardest winter for many years was particularly felt on the

Cotswolds. The situation became so bad at Brize that a large snow-blower was flown over from the States in a C-133 Cargomaster.

In the following year the numbers of KC-135s increasèd at Brize to support US Tactical Air Command operations. It was, aeronautically speaking, an exciting period. Various intelligence gathering and reconnaissance aircraft kept arriving and, in January 1964, great excitement was caused when a B-58 Hustler landed on a training flight.

Local inhabitants had become accustomed, but were always excited when the Americans pulled yet another aeronautical wonder out of the bag. There were rumours that Hustlers would replace the B-47s, but this was not to be. On 8 June 1964 an announcement was made that Brize Norton would return to the RAF in April 1965.

The US Air Force continued their Reflex Action operations right up to 1 April 1967. They also maintained an intense programme of alerts, exercises and visits, with many of the latter including strange aircraft. Locals still recall a U-2 which looked like an alien machine as it descended from the earth's stratosphere to England's Cotswolds.

Other local memories of the American involvement were smoke screen exercises and crash procedures. The smoke was produced by burning what the Yanks called 'fog oil', causing thick evil-smelling fumes to drift across the fair countryside.

Brize Norton — like Fairford, Greenham Common and Upper Heyford — attracted the anti-nuclear Committee of One Hundred, and was the scene of many demonstrations. To protect the Station from 'Ban the Bomb' marches, 2000 RAF Regiment troops moved in from 6 December 1961 onwards. Fortunately nothing serious occurred.

In retrospect — now that we have seen how the Soviet threat suddenly crumbled — it would seem that the Allies, especially the Americans, got it right. No-one doubted the sincerity of the demonstrators, yet all these USAF and RAF efforts, sustained over decades, paid off in the end.

The RAF returned to Brize Norton in 1965, first under the aegis of Transport Command, shortly afterwards to be renamed Air Support Command. Although the Americans had generously developed the airfield, much redevelopment was required for an entirely different aviation ballgame.

Brize now needed the facilities to handle large transport aircraft, and particularly their cargoes, both human and freight. Work went swiftly forward on a passenger terminal and a cargo handling shed. The pan or waterfront — as the main parking area was called — was fitted with full floodlighting. The large scale construction programme included living accommodation for Station personnel and a hotel for the needs of those in transit.

The most impressive item was a hangar designed to house up to six large aircraft. At the time of its completion, in August 1967, it was the largest cantilever structure in Western Europe. This building, known as Base Hangar, plays a very important part in life at Brize Norton, and its activities will be covered in a subsequent chapter.

From 1967 there was a steady build-up of personnel and facilities to make Brize into the principal strategic transport Station of the Royal Air Force. The resident Squadrons were No.10, operating VC10s; No.53, flying Belfasts; and Nos.99 and 511 with Britannias.

On 1 October 1968 Brize's new terminal building was opened and on-stream to provide a smooth flow of Service passengers to anywhere in the world. At the same time the Station continued with the essential task of moving bulk cargoes wherever required. An interesting sideline was the transfer of rare aircraft from various parts of the world for the RAF's magnificent museum at Hendon, North London.

Parallel with these activities, Brize's nearby sister base — RAF Lyneham in Wiltshire — built up its turboprop transport fleet of sixty Hercules. Such build-ups depend on available space as well as logistics. By early 1970 the Hercules fleet at

A No.53 Squadron Belfast freighter at Brize Norton. This was a very popular aircraft among RAF crews.

Lyneham was completed causing two Britannia Squadrons, No.99 and 511, to move to Brize Norton. They took up residence on the old B-47 sites to the south side of the airfield.

In 1974, thousands of Service personnel had to be evacuated at very short notice from trouble-torn Cyprus. Over an intensive 12 days, the Brize Squadrons flew 95 sorties and brought over 7500 men, women and children back to the UK. There seems to be a pattern of such Service efforts being succeeded by cutbacks. Later that year the Belfasts and Britannias were disposed of and their Squadrons run down. All these changes left Brize as a large airfield with few aircraft.

Fortunately, once the tide has ebbed it has to come in again. During 1976 the following major Units moved to Brize Norton: No.1 Parachute Training School, No.38 Group Tactical Communications Wing, the Joint Air Transport Establishment and the RAF Movements School. All have remained there to this day, and the important parts they have played in the many Brize achievements will be described later.

The late 70s saw RAF Brize Norton settling down to the mastering of several new roles. The base began to handle foreign visiting aircraft, and during this period more than 30 different air forces were looked after. It also handled — and still does so — VIP flights. Brize-based aircraft and staff have been responsible for conveying the Royal Family, Prime Ministers and cabinet ministers to all parts of the globe.

Another interesting development at Brize Norton was the steady advancement of air-to-air refuelling techniques. By the late 70s the RAF was aware that it had to replace its ageing Victor K2 aircraft. At that time a significant number of VC10 aircraft came on the market — retired by various airlines. To use them might seem a retrograde step, but the Air Force has a genius for getting the best out of aircraft, as borne out by its successes with the Comets and Britannias. It was decided to purchase these surplus VC10s and base them at Brize where the RAF's usage of this type was already established.

It was a neat solution, though there seems to be an underlying principle of Service life that nothing goes to plan. While the VC10s were being converted at the nearby British Aerospace works at Bristol, Argentinian forces invaded the Falkland Islands.

As with other Service Establishments, RAF Brize Norton was put on immediate standby.

A No.10 Squadron VC10 coming in to land at Brize Norton.

This involved everyone in general at Brize and No.10 Squadron in particular. The prime role was to build an air bridge, initially to Ascension Island, for troops and equipment en route to the Falklands. All too soon the air bridge had to span the vast empty sweep of the South Atlantic.

The Argentinian invasion was on 29 March 1982. The first operation by No.10 Squadron was on 5 April. It was an inauspicious one, to bring back from Montevideo in Uruguay those Royal Marines who had been overwhelmed at Port Stanley. But after that the Squadron and Brize people showed what else they could do. Every eight hours a fully laden aircraft left the Cotswolds for Ascension Island. During that month, No.10 Squadron completed 40 operational flights.

In May there were 62 flights, and June saw 43 operations, the most memorable being the return of survivors from HMS *Sheffield*. As for July, the total number of sorties leapt to an incredible — one is tempted to say an impossible — 153!

Following the 1982 Falklands campaign, 1983 saw two major firsts at Brize Norton. The first of nine VC10 Tankers arrived, as did the first of eight TriStar wide-bodied aircraft. This meant crews needed training to operate them and Squadrons formed as organizational cores. By May 1984 No.101 Squadron took responsibility for the VC10 Tankers, and in November No.216 Squadron did the same for the TriStars.

The exploits of these and other Brize Norton Squadrons are covered elsewhere in this book. However, a few more firsts can be mentioned here. During 1986 Brize Norton VC10s, while significantly practising air-to-air refuelling of Tornado aircraft to the Gulf, also achieved the first in-flight refuelling of a passenger aircraft over Sicily. Then in 1987 a Brize VC10 set a new world record from London to Perth. It achieved this through in-flight refuelling over Cyprus and the Indian Ocean to touchdown in 16 hours.

Of the eight TriStars two have been converted to tankers while the others are used as passenger and freight transports. For example, the TriStars are used regularly for Service support flights to Mount Pleasant airfield in the Falklands.

In 1986 Brize Norton was honoured by a visit from HM Queen Elizabeth II, and in

1987 the Station provided the meeting place for Mrs Thatcher and Mr Gorbachev. By then this air base on the Cotswolds was 50 years old and still going strong.

By 1990 Brize was busier than ever with routine and special flights. The routine ones included Service links to Washington, Belize, the Falklands and elsewhere. The specials were anywhere VIPs had to go. Station duties, crew training, engineering, catering — all proceeded at a brisk pace. So brisk was the pace that, for the first time at an RAF air base, it was decided to resurface the runway by night to maintain flying by day. Through an inscrutable law, that was when Brize became really busy.

The worsening Gulf situation resulted in various UN-backed measures including the British response code-named Operation Granby. From August 1990 Brize Squadrons operated 24 hours a day. Just about everyone and everything Service-wise was wanted in the Middle East — tents, beds and bedding; rations, bottled water and medical equipment; arms, ammunition and armour — the lists seemed endless. Equally seemingly endless streams of Service men and women crossed the Cotswolds to converge on Brize.

In retrospect it is amazing that Operation Granby was tagged on to Brize Norton's heavy workload. How was it carried successfully forward? Well, by inspired planning and sheer hard work. During those early Granby days, both No.10 Squadron's VC10s and No.216 Squadron's TriStars doubled their normal operating rates. As for No.101 Squadron's nine VC10 Tankers, they went to the Gulf where, between mid-January 1991 when the war really started and end-February when it abruptly stopped, they exceeded their usual refuelling rate by 350%.

But that was only part of Brize's response to the situation. The Station needed more aircraft, and these were chartered from civil operators such as British Airways, Britannia, Sabena and even far-flung Cathay Pacific. The airfield resembled an international airport. Among the many different types present was a Kuwait Airways Jumbo.

An interesting item of those days was concerned with noise. Normally Brize, like other air bases, receives a steady flow of complaints. One would have thought that a much increased number of planes operating at all hours would cause the complaint count to rise. Instead it fell significantly and, in its place, the locals rallied round offering help and hospitality.

Also, at the time a resident of nearby Carterton remarked that he would not have been surprised to see a spaceship come in to land at Brize. What he did see was

An American C5 Galaxy arrives at Brize Norton to help with Gulf War transportation. Note crewman sitting on top.

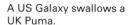

A US Galaxy swallows a UK Puma.

Russia's giant Antonov 124 — the Condor. This was needed to take some extra-large gear to the Gulf. It did so impeccably, the Russian-speaking crew using RAF callsigns. In addition, American C5s came and went, moving the heaviest and most awkwardly shaped articles. The sheer weight and volume of Operation Granby traffic called for all the help Brize could get.

Let us look a little closer at the problem. Every night some 50 or more fully-loaded pantechnicons climbed the Cotswolds to converge on RAF Brize Norton. Each load had to be sorted, shifted and stacked. Temporary hangars had to be erected for the relentlessly accumulating freight. There seemed never enough time, never enough people, yet the job was always done.

A Russian Antonov Condor arrives at Brize Norton, also to help with Gulf War transportation.

On the engineering side alone, 300 more people were needed during average Granby weeks, and 500 more at peak periods. Air Movements staff worked flat out

packing holds and cabins; then, compatible with safety, squeezing in yet more. Brize Norton's Movements Squadron, normally consisting of 150 staff, was augmented to 260 and achieved 1000% extra work.

While all this freight was being shifted, Brize Norton also delivered 30,000 Service personnel safely to the war zone. There was a reverse flow and thankfully only a trickle of wounded. Due to an inhospitable climate and hostile environment, mishaps occurred. Little was said of these illnesses and injuries at the time, but they had to be dealt with nevertheless. As desert exercises used live ammunition, there were gunshot wounds. Predictably there were broken limbs because, as one medic unsympathetically put it: 'Someone can always be relied on to fall off the back of a lorry.'

There were many other repercussions at Brize Norton because of the distant war. The No.1 Parachute Training School ceased training because there were no available aircraft out of which to parachute. That released help for the Station guard force, and for other support and supply duties. There was so much to do every Wing, Squadron, Section and Unit welcomed all comers.

Newcomers were likewise welcomed. Five hundred Americans were somehow housed in Brize Norton's married quarters when nearby RAF Little Rissington was converted into a hospital. Extra hands helped with the fitting and testing of NBC suits — protective clothing for nuclear, biological and chemical warfare.

Then there were the 'headless' families due to some 300 Brize fathers being away at the Gulf. It was essential their anxious wives and children should not be forgotten. After all, they were part of the larger RAF family. For a start, Gateway House — although busy looking after passengers in transit — decided to put on special Sunday lunches for the mums and kids. Entertainers were brought in, outings organized and free theatre tickets for top West End shows made available. These practical steps helped to keep up morale.

Meanwhile, Brize kept up its normal duties. Service Establishments in Europe, the Med, Central America and the South Atlantic were still supported. Important people continued to arrive at and depart from the Station. Up to 80 media representatives at a time were tolerantly controlled as they fought for news items and camera positions.

During the build-up of Operation Granby, Brize Norton moved over 1000 Service people a day from the Cotswolds to ten airfields around the Gulf. What Brize's own people did out there will be covered later. Suffice it to say here that Brize counted them out, and counted them in, through the base rightly referred to as the Gateway to the World.

Since then, life at RAF Brize Norton continues to be busy. Every day passengers and freight are on the move. The regular workload is handled without fuss, as are emergencies and rush jobs. Carrying problems that could be a crisis elsewhere are handled with a 'can do' attitude which converts them into solutions. Senior government figures and high ranking officers pass quietly through the place. Visiting aircraft are warmly welcomed.

Summing up, the Brize phenomenon is a bit of a paradox. It is efficient, yet laid back. It is a place where timing can be split second, yet there is a strange atmosphere of timelessness. A short drive, a brief cycle ride or a leisurely walk away and this hive of activity is lost amid windblown fields and lines of ancient trees extending to high horizons. Even the mightiest of its machines, to quote a poet from nearby Stratford-on-Avon, is all too soon 'vanished into air'.

Chapter 3

LOCAL INHABITANTS

RAF Brize Norton can be likened to a well-functioning, highly adaptable machine designed to take on a wide range of tasks — often several simultaneously — and to carry out each task with equal unfailing efficiency.

Many people will view the place as a single machine, which in one way it is. However, those who understand machinery will appreciate how all parts must work together. The main drive shafts are important, but so are oil seals and even the humblest clip.

This chapter will outline the chief components of the Brize Norton machine, and the next will describe both their locations and inter-relationships. Succeeding chapters will then tell how tasks are performed and what has been achieved over the years. As the RAF is about flying, we start with the Operations Wing and the flying Squadrons, then go on to those supporting or working with them.

Operations Wing

The Operations Wing at RAF Brize Norton primarily consists of an HQ element containing three Squadrons named Operations, Flying Support and Air Movements. Apart from running these three Squadrons, Ops Wing co-ordinates the work of various support Units and civil agencies required to sustain the operational task as well as those flying and ground Units undertaking the task itself. The work of this key wing is described at length in Chapter 7 'MOVERS AND COMMUNICATORS'. Suffice it to mention here that the Operations Wing moves 15,000 passengers and 400 tons of freight every month on a 24 hours a day, 365 days a year, basis.

No.10 Squadron

'Ten' is Brize Norton's longest serving Squadron and justly proud of the honour. It was formed at Farnborough on 1 January 1915, equipped with BE2C light bombers, and all too swiftly left for France where it operated with distinction throughout that grim war. No.10 Squadron continued giving solid service during World War II operating Whitleys, then Halifaxes. Notable missions included the great bomber raids, a part in the sinking of the *Tirpitz*, and attacks on the 'V' rocket sites.

In 1945, flying Dakotas, No.10 Squadron experienced its first taste of air transportation in India and the Berlin Airlift. There followed a brief reversion to bomber roles with Canberras and Victors until 1966 when the Squadron was re-equipped with VC10 C1 transport aircraft.

No.10 Squadron has proved the strength and versatility of the VC10 in emergency evacuations from Cyprus, Angola and Iran, also with UN peace-keeping forces in the

Above Pilots of No.10 Squadron in France 1918.

Above right Visit of three Kings (George V, Edward VIII and George VI) to No.10 Squadron in 1935.

troubled Middle East. In 1982 the Squadron carried troops and equipment to and from the Falklands. Today the VC10 continues to carry all three Services all over the world.

Another No.10 Squadron commitment is the carriage of VIPs. It has often been the Squadron's privilege to carry Her Majesty the Queen and other members of the Royal Family. The Prime Minister and other government officials are also frequent passengers.

The fitting of air-to-air refuelling probes has greatly increased the range and flexibility of the VC10s. In 1987 No.10 Squadron established two world records for direct flights to and from the Falkland Islands. The installation of refuelling pods is further increasing VC10 capability.

No.10 Squadron's motto is 'Rem Acu Tangere' meaning 'To Hit the Mark'. This

Winston Churchill inspects No.10 Squadron in 1942.

reflects its original bomber role, and during the Gulf crisis the Squadron immediately took on the task of outloading bombs. It also delivered personnel and spares. Somehow No.10 Squadron maintained its regular flight schedules — to Dulles and Belize among others — while fully meeting Gulf War requirements. A final interesting point on No.10. Each of its VC10 aircraft is named after a holder of the Victoria Cross.

Post-war aircraft flown by Nos.10 and 101 Squadrons included Canberras.

No.101 Squadron

Again it is necessary to go back to World War I since No.101 Squadron was formed on 12 July 1917. Equipped with FE2bs, it moved to France that August and operated over the Western Front until the Armistice. During the 20s and 30s the Squadron

A Victor tanker refuelling a Buccaneer, with a Phantom next in the queue.

Old and new. A Sopwith fighter with a Victor bomber and pilots in appropriate flying gear.

A VC10 in its role of passenger transport.

flew Boulton Paul Sidestrands and Overstrands, the latter with large moveable gun turrets. A castle turret is shown on the Squadron badge and the motto is 'Mens Agitat Molem' or 'Mind over Matter'.

Just before World War II No.101 Squadron was re-equipped with Blenheims. Wellingtons followed in 1941, and Lancasters in 1942. During both World Wars a total of 1129 men lost their lives while serving with the Squadron — 20 in the first and 1,109 in the second.

Post-war, No.101 Squadron operated Lincolns, Canberras and Vulcans in turn. As air-to-air refuelling became part of Squadron training, 101 crews took it to heart. They then demonstrated their mastery of the technique by flying three Vulcan B1s to

A VC10 in tanker role refuelling a Phantom.

Australia non-stop in less than 18 hours.

That was in 1963. In 1984, No.101 acquired five VC10 K2s converted from civilian aircraft, and in 1985 received four larger VC10 K3s converted from Super VC10s. Today the Squadron's main tanker tasks are to support the RAF's fast jets. Although this is primarily a UK air defence role, No.101 has taken part in numerous overseas exercises worldwide and broken more records.

For example, in 1986 a 101 Squadron aircraft made the first ever mid-air refuelling of a fully-laden passenger plane, and in 1987 celebrated its 70th Anniversary with yet another record. Squadron planes, using air refuelling, again flew non-stop to Australia in less than 16 hours. Thus they knocked two hours off their previous world record.

No.101 Squadron has an affinity with Australia. During 1988 the Squadron took part in the Five Nations exercise (involving Australia, New Zealand, Malaysia, Singapore and UK). These far- flung Air Forces have continued their co-operation and it is not unknown to see their aircraft at Brize, parked outside 101 Head-quarters.

No.101 Squadron's nine tanker VC10s began operating in the Gulf area from day one of that crisis. They did so from airfields at Thumrait, Seeb and Bahrain, finally moving to Riyadh. During one period they were flying 12 missions each night with all that implies in effort, professionalism and sheer hard work. There is also a lot more to the technical side of the Squadron's VC10 K3 to be covered in Chapter 6.

No.216 Squadron

Once again one must go back in time to World War I for the formation of the third Brize Squadron. In April 1918 No.16 Squadron was formed from elements of the Royal Naval Air Service's No.16 Squadron to become the RAF's No.216 Squadron. Hence the tradition of calling it 'Two-Sixteen'.

Two-Sixteen was initially equipped with Handley Page 0/400 night bombers, and after the Armistice was transferred to the Middle East. There the Squadron flew a variety of bomber aircraft — De Havilland DH10s, and also the Vickers Vimy, Victoria and Valentia — mainly on transport duties. During World War II No.216 continued its transport role, moving other Squadrons around the Middle East and

No.216 Squadron lines up in front of a TriStar.

Greece. They dropped airborne forces on Aegean Islands and moved detachments to Burma in 1944 to resupply the 14th Army. It was all unglamorous, but tough and essential work. After the war the Squadron continued with Air Transport flying in the Middle East, and in 1949 the Dakotas, with 216 since 1943, were replaced by Vickers Valettas.

In November 1955 No.216 Squadron returned to the United Kingdom and by June 1956 began taking delivery of De Havilland Comet 2 aircraft to become the first military jet transport Squadron in the world. In February 1962 it was also equipped with the larger Comet 4Cs. For close on 20 years the RAF in general, and Two-Sixteen in particular, showed what these aircraft could achieve. In 1975 the Squadron disbanded, but was re-formed briefly between 1979 and 1980 flying Buccaneers.

A TriStar fitted with a nose fuel-receiving probe and an under-fuselage fuel dispensing hose.

A TriStar being refuelled. Note airmen on left carrying out tests on fuel before it enters the aircraft.

Following the Falklands conflict it was decided to form a Squadron of strategic tanker aircraft. The Squadron chosen was Two-Sixteen and the aircraft the Lockheed TriStar, with six coming initially from British Airways and later three more from Pan-Am. Currently the Squadron has the former as passenger/transports and two of the latter as tankers on its strength. The Squadron is thus well equipped to carry out both worldwide air transport and air-to-air refuelling duties well into the twenty-first century.

Meanwhile Two-Sixteen's aerial activities are so diverse it is difficult to pick out the specials. Perhaps this is because the Squadron seems to specialize in specials. Special care was given to ex-POWs and widows visiting former battlefields and war graves in the Far East, and disaster relief for Chile is another example. The Squadron

Below left A view of a Rolls-Royce RB211 tail engine in a TriStar.

Below Control room of the ringmain fuel system at Brize Norton.

has also visited countries as far apart as Australia, Japan, Kenya and New Zealand. It maintains a regular schedule to Cyprus as well as Ascension Island and the Falkland Islands. Its tankers provide refuelling support for Tornados, Harriers and Jaguars on their way to Cyprus, the Middle East and North America. And in 1988, No.216 Squadron was closely involved in Operation Golden Eagle taking Tornados round the world.

As for the Gulf War, Two-Sixteen was heavily tasked from the start, and every month exceeded 150% of their normal flying time. In addition to its heavy involvement in air transport operations, crews also participated in air-to-air refuelling during Desert Storm. Following that, the Squadron has run freighter flights to Riyadh and Jubayl while returning to its other duties in support of the South Atlantic forces and those in Cyprus.

No.241 Operational Conversion Unit

If one has to allocate priorities, the RAF is primarily about flying, with training coming a close second. Indeed, some will argue — especially those going on yet another course — that training tends to predominate. Undoubtedly, training is the secret of success, and the motto of Brize Norton-based No.241 Operational Conversion Unit (OCU) could not be simpler. It reads 'Teach Well'.

This Unit began its days in September 1944 as No.1332 Heavy Conversion Unit (HCU), training crews for York aircraft. It became No.241 OCU in January 1948, by which time its aircraft had progressed to Halifaxes and Hastings. 1950 saw the phasing out of the York. Meanwhile, all of No.241 OCU's aircraft and crews did more than their fair share of work during the Berlin Airlift.

The important stage in the history of the OCU occurred in 1965 when Brize Norton was handed back from the USAF to the RAF. The main requirement then was training crews for the VC10s of No.10 Squadron which became operational with these aircraft in mid-1966. In 1970 the OCU became responsible for training Belfast and Britannia crews, as well as those for the VC10.

While emphasis is given in this book to the aircraft — VC10s and TriStars — currently operated at Brize, it must also be mentioned in the history of No.241 OCU that crew training for many other planes took place, all involving meticulous work and requiring high standards both for trainers and trainees.

January 1982 saw the formation of yet another No.241 OCU training flight for the VC10 tanker crews of No.101 Squadron. Later that year, Unit personnel were themselves involved in the campaign for recapturing the Falkland Islands. Then in September 1985 TriStar air steward training courses began for No.216 Squadron. Today the Operational Conversion Unit trains new crews (and retrains old crews) for VC10 transport and tanker aircraft, as well as teaching flight refuelling techniques to air and ground crews, and to other air forces. This Brize Unit is known worldwide, and other services are always eager to attend its courses.

Joint Air Transport Establishment (JATE)

JATE is the acronym of an important Unit situated at the south side of Brize Norton. It could be called a think tank for Armed Services transportation. It is tasked by the Ministry of Defence to solve air transport problems and improve airborne capabilities. JATE is truly joint-Service, having a colonel as commandant, a wing commander as deputy and staff from the Royal Navy, Army, RAF and Royal Marines all working together in one Unit.

This Establishment uses the latest technology to turn ideas into reality. Computer-aided design, technical authors, graphic artists and fully equipped workshops are all available at JATE, as well as word processing and publishing facilities. Because of its unique formation and resources, JATE is a recognized authority on air transport matters, publishing many definitive documents. Aircraft and helicopter loading data, trim sheets and guides to the design of air transport equipment are all produced by JATE.

The advice and expertise available at JATE has been recognized by many civilian companies, and the Establishment's resources and reputation make it an ideal focal point for the evaluation of new ideas and techniques. The Unit provides design guidance, product evaluation and feasibility studies. Its siting at Brize — the hub of the Services air transport system — is a practical location for a very practical Unit.

Tactical Communications Wing

Originally this Unit was formed to support aircraft when they were absent from their home bases. The bird on the wing badge — a rock dove which was the ancestor of the homing pigeon — neatly conveys the problems of deployment. The many problems are too numerous to list here but, when they are analysed, all come down to communications. The Wing's primary role therefore is to provide field contacts and navigational aids to the Navy, Army and Air Force. Its communication Units have specialists and equipment capable of operating over thousands of miles.

For example when the RAF is working with the Royal Navy, the Wing communicates with ships at sea. Similarly, as but one instance, when working with the Army, special techniques are used to guide Harrier aircraft back to their forest hides. TCW technicians provide repair facilities for radio equipment and airfield aids. These vary from office to office and often tent to tent. They are very practical people and can transform a deserted airstrip into a fully-equipped airfield for instant attack, transport and helicopter capabilities.

Throughout its history the Tactical Communications Wing has been actively involved in key exercises and operations — the Zambian oil lift in 1965, Nepal famine relief in 1972, the Belize conflict 1977, the Falklands in 1982 and the Gulf War in 1991 — to list some of their major contributions.

Brize Radar

Brize Radar is a unique air traffic control system providing area and terminal services from the same Unit. Thus the Unit reports directly to the AOC Military Air Traffic Operations for area functions and to the Brize Station Commander concerning airfield and aircraft. The amalgamation arose owing to the overcrowding of Oxfordshire air space — arguably the most congested area in the UK. The air traffic controllers have to deal with everything that flies, from light club aircraft to wide-bodied planes, including many visiting planes.

They accomplish this with a primary radar and a selection of secondary radar which sweep a radius of 80 nautical miles from ground level to 24,000 ft. An airways crossing service is provided, also a centralized approach service for nine nearby airfields including Fairford and Kemble. A glance at a map of southern England will show that a place called Heathrow also comes into the picture.

In total, the Brize Radar controllers and assistants deal with over 100,000 aircraft movements a year. It is a never-ending as well as a demanding and intensive task. Strangely enough, air traffic controllers are always very cheerful people, the constant challenges of the job bringing their own rewards.

RAF Movements School

The RAF Movements School sited at Brize Norton is an independent Unit tasked directly by the Ministry of Defence. The function of the School is to provide every aspect of air and surface movements training for selected officers of the Supply Branch, students from foreign and Commonwealth forces and all air movements airmen. Other RAF personnel, also those from the Royal Navy and Army, attend the School courses.

The subject of air movements is a complex and ever-changing one. During a typical training year, the School runs many different types of courses and delivers 130 of them to some 1400 students. Practical training is given with VC10 and Hercules freight load simulator mock-ups. The School teaches a range of automation systems, including passenger reservation, checking-in and load planning.

In addition to a packed training programme, the RAF Movements School at Brize runs courses both during the evenings and weekends for the nearby No.4624 (County of Oxford) Royal Auxiliary Air Force Movements Squadron covered later in this chapter. Such a School has been in existence for 40 years and has seen many changes. The RAF 'Movements', as it is called, combines both the fundamental principles of air movements with the latest methods available for transporting people and freight worldwide.

Aircraft Engineering Squadron

The non-stop work performed by this Squadron to keep Brize aircraft flying will have a chapter of its own (Chapter 5 'BASE HANGAR'). As the Base Hangar is such a landmark, not only on the Station, but also in the district, it must be mentioned here. When the hangar opened on 16 August 1967, it was the largest in Europe and cost £50 million.

The hangar is built to a unique cantilever design with all the load being taken by the office side of the structure. The building weighs 3000 tons and is held together by 25,000 high tensile bolts. When the wind blows, a lift effect is given to the roof, thus reducing loading on the main support girders.

An interesting point the designers had to take into account was the weight of snow — not unknown on the Cotswolds. They calculated that eight inches of snow on the roof would render it in danger of collapsing, so this is countered by heating. An outside boiler house serves to heat the hangar and roof via 11 miles of pipes.

The huge hangar interior of 20,180,750 cubic ft can take up to six Brize transport aircraft at a time for maintenance and overhauls. The Base Hangar is an engineering Station within a Station, another world of expertise vital to flying operations.

No.1 Parachute Training School

The country's Parachute Training School came into being during the dark days of mid-1940 at the express instructions of Prime Minister Winston Churchill. The first aircraft to be used was a Bomber Command Whitley, which was far from ideal. A 28 ft diameter parachute was also used and operated by a line attached to a strong point of the aircraft. That, too, was not ideal, but it was a beginning.

By the end of 1940 some 2000 descents were made, and the first drop 'for real' took place in February 1941 on an Italian aqueduct. Gradually the School spread its sphere of influence, and during the war years other similar parachute Schools were set up in the Mediterranean, Middle East and India. By 1944 the Dakota was primarily used for drops, though this aircraft was not the optimum. Nevertheless, Allied soldiers of many nations passed through the Schools and took part in the key assaults on Sicily, Normandy, Arnhem and the Rhine Crossing.

After the war No.1 Parachute Training School moved to RAF Upper Heyford, then to Abingdon and finally to Brize Norton. It continued to be the foremost parachute School in Europe and, apart from training UK personnel, other nations sent their soldiers to become parachutists, and even instructors. A series of

Early stage of learning to become a paratrooper.

improvements were made — double door jumping, free falling and steerable parachuting. A free fall display team became an integral part of the School, and its members the world-famous Falcons.

In 1967, the Hercules, capable of dropping parachutists in one 'stick', proved to be the most suitable aircraft for this aerial art, and it still is. On 6 March 1969 18-year-old Private Blunn made the School's millionth descent from a Hercules and, in July 1971, No.1 PTS had the honour of training the Prince of Wales to make his first

RAF parachute jumping instructors show how it is done in full gear, carrying weapons and wearing oxygen masks.

AOC visits the crew of
No.19 Squadron RAF
Regiment missile fire Unit.

parachute descent. In 1978 Prince Charles returned to complete the full course accompanied by Prince Andrew. Both trained for two weeks and qualified for their parachute wings.

In 1985, the military version of the ram-air parachute was introduced for landing control. Techniques developed over the years have resulted in the ability to parachute by day or night 90 fully-equipped troops plus 3000 lb of stores on a single Hercules run over a drop zone. More about the No.1 Parachute Training School and its technique will be given in Chapter 8 'ATTACKERS AND DEFENDERS'.

The RAF Auxiliary
Regiment undergoing
exercises.

No.19 Squadron RAF Regiment

No.19 Squadron of the RAF Regiment is a lodger Unit at Brize Norton. Its role is to defend RAF Upper Heyford and RAF Fairford which are bases used by the US Air Force. This Squadron is the largest in terms of manpower, also it is the biggest of all the RAF Regiment's Rapier operatives having some 12 fire Unit detachments. Every year No.19 deploys to the Royal Artillery ranges in the Outer Hebrides for two weeks. There Rapier missile operators and controllers fire at fast, small targets with live missiles.

But this is the glamorous side of the Regiment's more mundane yet essential tasks. Its main task is to guard air bases. RAF Regiment history goes back to 1942 when incoming enemy aircraft were more of a threat than a land attack. Early Units manned anti-aircraft guns, were involved in countering the V-1 flying bomb threat to London, and later moved to NW Europe clearing pockets of German resistance in the wake of the Allied armies.

No.19 Squadron RAF Regiment has participated in several UK and NATO exercises both at home and overseas. In order to counter very low-level, all-weather aircraft, the Squadron is equipped, as mentioned above, with British Aerospace Rapier missiles and Marconi Blindfire Radar Tracker systems. How the Squadron is organized and operates will be covered, with the Parachute School, in Chapter 8.

No.244 Signal Squadron (Disbanded July 1992)

Known as The Red Hand Gang for reasons to be explained, No.244 Signal Squadron was another of those Brize Norton Units quietly performing essential tasks on the base and elsewhere. In fact each of its personnel spent more than 150 days annually on detached duties which, in the last decade, took them to over 30 different countries.

The Unit was formed by the War Office early in World War II after learning the advantages of close Army/Air Force co-operation so successfully practised by the Germans. It soon became apparent that there was an urgent need for the Unit's vehicles to carry an immediate identifiable sign, and its commander, for lack of anything better, chose the Red Hand from his family armorial sign. He was a McNeil and a direct descendant from the Kings of Ulster. Over the years, War Office officials frowned over the Red Hand, but the Gang persuaded them that performance justified it.

So the Red Hand sign was seen through the North African and Italian campaigns, the Normandy invasion and post-war in German-based NATO forces. In its final form, No.244 Signal Squadron at Brize was part of the RAF's Tactical Communications Wing providing air support liaison for airborne brigades, infantry divisions and helicopter forces.

County of Oxford Squadrons

Two Royal Auxiliary Air Force Squadrons — No.2624 Regiment and No.4624 Movements — are based at Brize. Their personnel are local people wishing to help ease the regular Station workload and particularly to assist during periods of natural emergency, including war.

No.2624 (County of Oxford) Squadron Royal Auxiliary Air Force Regiment is a direct descendent of a Unit formed in 1943. It operated in Britain, North Africa, Corsica, Sardinia and over the Italian mainland then moved to Yugoslavia, France and elsewhere on 'special duties' until disbandment in 1945. Today the Squadron's role is to reinforce overseas Station defence forces. It trains auxiliaries, which includes visits to camps and ranges both at home and overseas. Adventure training — such as climbing, parachuting, surfing and skiing are encouraged.

No.4624 (County of Oxford) Royal Auxiliary Air Force Movements Squadron dates its formation back to 1924. At peak periods there were 65 auxiliary Squadrons of which 14 took part in the Battle of Britain. The first enemy aircraft shot down in the battle was accomplished by an Auxiliary fighter pilot. After a fine war record and many detachments, No.4624 was formed at Brize in 1982 to provide a pool of fully-trained movements personnel. The Squadron is fully operational and has proved itself in times of intense activity, such as during the Gulf War.

No.2267 (Brize Norton) Air Training Corps

Many people tend to overlook the importance and youthful enthusiasms of ATC Units throughout the country. It is in these Units that bright boys and girls are encouraged to learn about the RAF and even make it a career. They can become cadets between the ages of 13 and 20, they meet two evenings a week and they are offered an inspiring range of activities. These include flying, gliding, shooting and adventure training. There are also valuable courses on aviation subjects — all free.

At Brize Norton the normal Corps strength is 50 cadets. There used to be mostly boys, but in recent equal opportunity years the numbers of girls have grown. Moreover, they have proved to be bright and dedicated. With women pilots and navigators now making their way in the Air Force, the men will have to try harder to keep ahead. No.2267 Squadron ATC at RAF Brize Norton is a particularly active Unit and its members are encouraged to participate in the life of the Station.

No.1 Group Mobile Servicing Section

1991 saw the disbandment of a Brize section which deserves mention here. No.1 Group MSS was a small group of highly experienced and dedicated aircraft engineers — 20 in total — who lived locally and would go instantly to help out anywhere in the UK or the world. The Group was formed in 1953 to relieve regular personnel when

An inspection of No.2267 (Brize Norton) Air Training Corps.

pressures became intense. The Section operated in four or five man teams supporting mixed transport movements. Despite being based at Brize with its VC10 and TriStar aircraft, all members were trained for and qualified on Hercules at nearby Lyneham. They also helped other air forces and airlines who were in a tight spot.

Over the years, No.1 Group MSS has supported NATO forces, taken part in exercises; learned about foreign aircraft, equipment and techniques; also ground equipment, heating, lighting and air-conditioning systems. During the Falklands Campaign, the Section handled more than 1000 aircraft flying to and from the South Atlantic at Dakar. During the Gulf War, team members and their tool kits were busy at Dhahran and Thumrait initially, then later at Jubayl, Tabuk, Bahrain, Riyadh, Qaisumah and Kuwait itself. Everyone meeting them, or even knowing them, has spoken highly of their exploits. They represent the British art of improvisation — quietly yet successfully applied — at its best.

Now, having introduced some, though not all, of RAF Brize Norton's local inhabitants, the time has come to walk round the Station, to see how they fit and work together.

Above left Catching them young at RAF Brize Norton.

Above Husband and wife air steward team.

Chapter 4

GUIDED TOUR

Newcomers to RAF Brize Norton arrive either by air or via country lanes during the final stage of their land journey. From above, the main runway and taxiways predominate. At ground level the airfield seems to be missing — that is until a heavy jet transport suddenly thunders past the buildings.

There are two well-used ground approaches to Brize Norton. One is from Swindon railway station, as described in the opening chapter. The other is by the M40/A40 out of West London. After by-passing High Wycombe, the motorway dips into the huge cutting near Stokenchurch and crosses a broad vale towards Oxford. The university city is also by-passed and soon afterwards the road begins to rise again. The old Cotswold wool town of Witney is likewise by-passed and, almost immediately, the signs to RAF Brize Norton begin. There is a selection of lanes to the left all somehow leading to the Station.

The village of Brize Norton itself is but one of the many stone-built hamlets surrounding the Station, yet the closest to it. The scene is picturesque and the atmosphere sleepy until another of those heavy jet transports passes overhead. Carterton adjoining the Station is entirely different. It is a bustling town as active in the small hours as during the day. Cars come and go. Airmen and airwomen cycle past in droves, on their way to hundreds of tasks around the Station. The local inhabitants think RAF because they mainly are RAF. They are at least very air-minded or they would not be living there. So this guided tour should begin in Carterton before entering the Station.

The clue to Carterton lies in the variety of its houses. These vary from adequate fabricated apartments to comfortable country homes set in their own well-kept gardens. The majority of people living in them are either RAF personnel or civilians connected in one way or another with the Station. Single airmen and airwomen tend to live on the Station; couples outside. They live very full social lives because there is a great deal going on all the time. They are also extremely mobile. Apart from their own mobility, everyone knows and accepts that he or she may have to take off for anywhere in the world at any time.

Despite differences in ranks and trades, this is a truly classless society. The three ladders leading upward for everyone are those of character, ability and experience. It is as fair as life can be fair. Talking at random to citizens of Carterton reveals they are airmen technicians, Corporal cooks, Sergeant Loadmasters, pilots and navigators or ex-RAF retired and still 'helping out'. Young boys tell of Dad being in Colorado or Cyprus. Old boys proudly relate how they used to assemble Horsa gliders or worked with the United States Air Force, affectionately known as the Yanks.

Thus Carterton is a Service-orientated town. There is a NAAFI Families Shop situated in it. The facility includes a fresh meat butchery, a fine fruit and vegetable

section, a large gifts and durables area including kiddies' clothing, a comprehensive range of frozen foods and a delivery service. There are also a video library and a cafeteria within the complex. Further services include car, caravan and boat sales; household, personal and holiday insurance, photography, jewellery and Interflora. Additionally, the NAAFI operates another shop inside Brize Norton Station. Both shops are open every day of the week.

Within walking distance of the main NAAFI in Carterton there are two more supermarkets and essential shops such as:

Above left Corporal Vicky Stevenson, the first female dog handler in the RAF, with Bismark.

Bakers	Insurance Companies
Bank	Jewellers
Building Societies	Licensed Betting Shop
Butchers	Motor Spares
Chemists	Newsagents
Clothes	Off Licences
Coffee Shop	Opticians
Do-It-Yourself	Post Offices
Dry Cleaners	Records and Tapes
Electrical	Shoe Repairer
Estate Agents	Sports Goods
Florists	Tailors
Fish and Chips	Take Away Foods
Gift Shop	Tobacconists
Greengrocers	Toy Shop
Greeting Cards	Travel Agents
Hairdressers	Video Hire
Indian Restaurant	Washeteria

Most needs for everyday living are catered for around Carterton crossroads, while nearby Witney has yet more shops including branches of the larger multiple stores. Moreover, the base is within easy reach of Cheltenham, Oxford and Swindon.

Above Briefing of guards at RAF Brize Norton.

One of the five soccer
pitches at Brize Norton.

So much for shops. What about education? To start with, there are four primary Schools in Carterton, including a Roman Catholic one. There are also two secondary Schools — or rather colleges — one at Carterton and the other at nearby Burford. All Oxfordshire secondaries are comprehensive and it is Local Education Authority policy to give parents as much freedom of choice and opportunity as possible. Service children are welcome because they are bright and adaptable.

Then there are the evening classes, the technical and commercial courses, adult educational facilities and the library services. Libraries are available in Carterton and on Brize Norton Station. Carterton stocks about 24,000 books, Brize 7000. The Station Library has new books and bestsellers as well as reference books, textbooks and most periodicals. This emphasis on education and training permeates the Air Force because modern day aviation activities depend on A-levels and degrees.

How does RAF Brize Norton fare on the sporting side? There are two major sports fields within the Station, providing two cricket pitches, two rugby pitches, two hockey pitches, five football pitches and eight tennis courts. After those come the indoor facilities including badminton, basketball, netball, volleyball and squash. There is a fully-equipped gym, a large swimming pool, a 12-lane bowling alley and even a dry ski slope. The following is a list of sports available to all Brize personnel and, wherever possible, their dependents:

Angling	Cycling	Netball	Swimming
Archery	Equitation	Parachuting	Tennis
Athletics	Football	Rowing	Table Tennis
Badminton	Flying	Rugby	Tenpin Bowling
Basketball	Gliding	Sailing	Tug-of-War
Boxing	Golf	Shooting	Volleyball
Canoeing	Hockey	Skiing	Windsurfing
Cross Country	Judo	Squash	
Cricket	Motor Sports	Sub Aqua	

The list speaks for itself so, having outlined the various social amenities and social activities, the time has come to describe the actual Station. For visitors and contractors there is but one entrance and exit. Strict security begins once past a welcoming flowerbed.

The twelve-lane bowling alley at Brize Norton — largest in the RAF.

From there a side road leads to Gateway House, as described in Chapter 1, while ahead lies the Station's main thoroughfare. On the way round there will be Hastings Drive, Anson Avenue and Argosy Road with their aircraft connotations, also Halton Road and Cranwell Avenue outside the Station. The complex of roads and buildings set amid spacious lawns and thick trees gives the impression of a college campus.

Immediately to the left of the main thoroughfare into Brize is the Station's

The snack bar at the bowling alley.

WRAF netball team.

Mechanical Transport Squadron. Lined up outside workshops are those various vehicles necessary to keep a big air base mobile — from small hatchback runabouts to coaches, cranes, trucks, low-loaders and aircraft tugmasters. All in all, the Mechanical Transport Squadron has, drives and maintains well over 700 vehicles.

The next two Station Units on either side of the main thoroughfare are the Supply Wing on the left, while the Education and Training Squadron is to the right. Both are Units, not so much necessary to visitors, but of high importance to Brize personnel. The Supply Wing sees to those millions of items without which Service life would

Boxing tuition and tournaments, one of many sports provided at Brize Norton.

Service children and swimming instructors at the Station pool.

come to a standstill. As for Education and Training, it is yet another gateway — towards self-betterment and promotion.

Simply noting a few items on the Supply Wing organization chart will indicate its overall responsibilities. The Domestic Supply Flight has a Warden looking after the curtains and carpets in the married quarters. This does not mean that Brize goes in for luxuries. Its curtains have to last eight years, and carpets twelve. However, electric bulbs and strip lights are replaced right away, provided the old one is produced. Details, perhaps, but efficient organizations are run on these.

The Supply Wing could make a book in itself, for all Service life is there. There are clothing stores open every weekday and a tailoring service. The laundry exchange point is next to the bedding stores and there are dry cleaning facilities. As Brize

Planes of Brize Norton Flying Club.

General view of MT operating compound. This section deals with Station support operations.

Norton is the RAF's major transport base, emphasis is placed on baggage services — for inbound and outbound luggage, the loan of packing cases, the use of removal firms.

As for Education and Training across the road, this provides advice and help on all aspects of these important subjects — from children's schooling to further education. Information covering trade tests, promotion exams, computer technology and language tuition is freely available. When an individual's education requirement cannot be met through local classes, learning packages are arranged, also there are residential courses at universities. Some of the latter are just up the road from Brize — at nearby Oxford — and many personnel have enhanced their careers and lifestyles at the world's most prestigious educational Establishment.

Once past Supply and Education, there are several side roads and walkways, again between lawns and under trees. To the left lie the headquarters of two flying Squadrons (Nos.10 and 216), also the Station workshops. Beyond can be seen the Passenger Terminal building and the Tactical Communications Wing hangars. Brize buildings are mostly constructed of a pleasant light brown brick, while hangars and

General view of airfield support parking area.

A flight simulator mobile platform at No.241 Operational Conversion Unit.

other metalwork are painted dark green.

At this point the main thoroughfare bends by another hangar which houses No.1 Parachute Training School. A visit will be made to the School in Chapter 8. On the other side of the road are the Flight Simulators on which Brize pilots are trained. These brown-clad buildings have a deceptively quiet appearance. Inside, however, they are busy places from early morning to late at night with trainees, instructors and simulator technicians working their way through programmes.

The main thoroughfare bends further by the office of the Parachute Training School. On the writer's first visit to Brize, his guide had just pointed out this building when its door opened and two soldiers emerged — both on crutches! So it will be interesting to learn what it takes to become a paratrooper.

Fortuitously, perhaps, the Station's Medical Centre is next door, as is the Dental Centre. These centres are more for on-Station personnel and those passing through, though all who need attention are treated. Both centres are open every day from 8.30 a.m. to 5 p.m. Routine examinations are normally by appointment, but there is an emergency service outside normal working hours. A major medical task for a Station such as Brize is that of handling many diverse inoculations and vaccinations. No appointments are needed for these. Anyone going to Outer Mongolia or up the Amazon is treated with the right jabs and/or tablets.

After the Medical and Dental Centres comes Administrative Wing Headquarters, from where the efforts of the largest support wing in the Station is co-ordinated. Admin covers just about everything — security and fire services, education, personnel, administration and accounting, catering, messes, accommodation (single and married) and the maintenance of the entire infrastructure of the Station. It also sees to the rewards and responsibilities, like the proverbial good and bad news. The first covers welfare, sports and entertainments. The second includes guard duties, parades and inspections. All these and more are contained in Admin-produced Station Standing Orders. The Information Handbook given to every Brize newcomer contains the following meaningful message:

Many of these orders will apply to you personally so make sure you are familiar with them and thus avoid the trouble that will undoubtedly follow should you fail to comply.

Above The Officers' Mess.

Personnel Management Squadron next door has three main Sections designated P1, P2 and P3. The P1 Section is responsible for all legal and disciplinary matters which, as one legal eagle put it, mostly involves unravelling personal problems. The P2 Section, known to old hands as the Golden Eagle, looks after officers' pay, allowances and personnel records, whilst P3 does the same for the airmen and airwomen. Interestingly enough, airmen under 18 years of age are paid fortnightly in cash, but are encouraged to open bank accounts. Barclays, Lloyds and Midland all have branches in Carterton.

The Station's Accounts Flight is also located in the Personnel Management building. This department deals with bills, claims and payments. It will be appreciated that a Station as busy as Brize involves accounting work which is both considerable and complicated. The specialist staff in Accounts have long learned how to support action-packed flying activities. They give advice to crews embarking on overseas flights, and duty staff are available to meet emergency demands outside normal working hours.

Administration Wing Headquarters is bracketed between the Officers' and Sergeants' Messes. The former looks out across the airfield and is a pleasant rather than a luxurious place. Apart from formal occasions, the atmosphere is relaxed and club-like. Junior officers in particular enjoy staying there, as it meets their basic needs for a room, food and drink, congenial company and especially a good selection of sports and social activities. In the evenings and at weekends they play tennis or squash, go canoeing or yachting, or fly club planes. They also have a lot of studying to do, and the place is conducive to working singly or in groups.

Sergeants' Messes throughout the RAF appear similar, though they have a subtle difference from Officers' Messes. To put it bluntly, Sergeants know how to look after themselves and their own. So, while the Officers' Mess has a slightly spartan air, that of the Sergeants enjoys every comfort. The best food, the best parties and, some say, the best company are to be found in the Sergeants' Messes. As one Brize Sergeant modestly remarked: 'Let's say we are no exception.'

Continuing on the main thoroughfare through RAF Brize Norton one passes a series of individual buildings set amid more lawns. On the left are the Fire Section, Gym and Physical Education Flight. To the right are the Station Church, Police and Security Flight. As previously indicated, Security is taken very seriously at this base which deals literally with all ranks to the highest in the land. Security affects every

Above right The Officers' Mess kitchen.

The Sergeants' Mess.

person either Stationed at or visiting the Station.

Speed limits are signposted throughout the Station. The general rule is 30 mph, dropping to 20 mph or even 10 mph in certain zones. 'Sleeping policemen' across all roads serve as reminders to drivers who tend to be heavy on accelerators. RAF Police vehicles maintain what they call 'a presence.'

Side roads off the main thoroughfare lead to Units such as the VC10 Maintenance School, No.4624 Squadron, married quarters for airmen and officers, and to Gateway Primary School. The main way continues to quarters for single airmen and airwomen, a large complex which includes the Junior Ranks Restaurant, Swimming Pool and Spotlight Club. This complex is almost another Station within a Station.

For those who knew the Royal Air Force of old, the greatest change wrought over the years has been the improved treatment of the Junior Ranks. Officers' Messes remain more or less the same, the Sergeants continue to do all right, thank you, whereas the upgrading of Junior Ranks' food, quarters and amenities is considerable. This view was put to a retired Group Captain who, no doubt recalling his earlier,

The Sergeants' Mess servery.

bleaker days, remarked: 'That is as it should be.'

The point is proved by a closer look at RAF Brize Norton's Junior Ranks Restaurant. There, two dining rooms, named the East Wing and West Wing, function as follows. The East Wing offers roast meals. It also has a Steak Bar and a Coffee Lounge. The West Wing has a Salad Bar serving freshly prepared dishes and a selection of health foods. Better still, there is a Gourmet Bar offering at least two different foreign dishes each day. In addition, the Main Servery in the West Wing provides up to half a dozen starters, main courses and sweets.

How does all this come about, not only at the Junior Ranks Restaurant, but throughout the base? The Station Messing Committee is made up of representatives from every Unit and meets regularly 'to improve gastronomic standards and cater for individual tastes.' Likewise, Catering Squadron personnel are dedicated to purchasing and preparing the best in food and drink, both for taste and health eating. They contribute their expertise to numerous special occasions such as anniversary celebrations, groups of visitors and, in particular, children's parties. The same high standards prevail at the nearby Spotlight Club which is open to all Junior Ranks and their families. The club maintains an on-going programme of family entertainment, including regular dances.

Talking about clubs, RAF Brize Norton has many others apart from the Sports Clubs previously mentioned. None of these is a class or rank-ridden Establishment. They are places where enthusiasts at all levels can pursue their special mutual interests. A few examples will show this.

There is a very active Theatre Club whose members put on their own plays as well as visit the best theatres in London, Oxford and elsewhere. There is the Model Aircraft Club which is keenly supported in that aviation-minded area. There is the Photographic Club with its own studio and darkroom. A Motor Club looks after touring and racing enthusiasts, and a Hobbies Club contains full woodworking, carpentry and other facilities. Brize's 12-lane bowling alley is the largest in the RAF, and all members of Service families are warmly welcome. As for youngsters, crowds of Cubs, Scouts and Guides, Brownies and Beavers, often pervade the place.

The Station produces a monthly magazine called Gateway. This contains news and articles from Squadrons, clubs and other organizations on the Station. It is distributed to all sections and married quarters free of charge. Local information is likewise contained in a 'Welcome' booklet which is in effect a family guide to Brize Norton and its environs.

So far this guided tour of RAF Brize Norton has been in and around the Station quarters. Beyond the Station (and three times as large) is the airfield. Apart from aircraft movements, it stretches quiet and empty into the far distance to blend with the surrounding Cotswolds. When people and vehicles move about Brize airfield they soon become mere dots. Only those who have work to do are allowed there. The rest of the Station and particularly the public are prohibited. One bona fide airfield inhabitant gave a couple of succinct reasons: 'We can't have happy families picnicking by the runway or kiddies turning on taps which deliver aviation fuel at over 500 gallons a minute.'

Nevertheless, let us set off round Brize airfield taking heed of the main runway and various taxiways, also making sure not to touch any taps. As with most large airfields, one cannot gain a true impression of it from the ground. Distance deceives. Only air crews and their passengers see Brize airfield as it really is, in plan form, but it can be visualized as follows.

Imagine a figure eight lying on its side with a long straight line passing horizontally through the centre and projecting at both ends. The loops of the figure eight are the perimeter taxiways and the line is the main runway. Its length is 10,000 ft and the direction practically east to west.

Returning to the image of a figure eight lying on its side, the Brize terminal building is sited near the top of the right hand loop. Taxiways from the pan lead down to the centre point of the main runway, or to either end, via a perimeter road. This road right round the airfield is used both by aircraft and those ground personnel driving to and from work at distant buildings. Observing a wide-bodied aircraft, such as a TriStar, taxiing towards one's car is like an ant's eye view of an approaching dinosaur. The aircraft passes, its powerful jet engines fill the air with noise, and the car rocks.

RAF and other approved personnel going on airfield duty generally head for the perimeter by a road past Gateway House and the Base Hangar. Suddenly the Station and its many buildings is replaced by a great expanse of grass, parking bays and glimpses of fuel sites. The last is like the tip of an iceberg because RAF Brize Norton has a fuel facility which is the most comprehensive and advanced of its kind in Europe.

Deep underground round the airfield are Bulk Fuel Installations (BFIs) and a Hydrant Refuelling System (HRS). A typical BFI has a capacity of over two million gallons and a battery of high speed pumps to refuel/defuel points at aircraft parking bays. The whole facility is computer controlled to monitor flow rates, pipe pressures and tank temperatures. Thus Brize aircraft are refuelled or defuelled with speed and accuracy, yet most of the technically sophisticated system is invisible.

As the perimeter road nears the eastern end of the main runway, traffic lights at red warn of aircraft movements which naturally take priority. A speck in the sky, also to the east, rapidly becomes a VC10. Once it has landed and turned toward the air terminal pan, the red traffic lights change to green and cars can proceed round the perimeter.

A miscellaneous line of buildings follows the south side of Brize airfield. The first building is occupied by No.19 Squadron RAF Regiment. The Regiment has an office in the Station itself, next to Education and Training. More will be told of No.19 in Chapter 8. After the RAF Regiment building come hangars and headquarters occupied by the Joint Air Transport Establishment. Notices outside indicated the various sections — Flying Training, Drawing Office, Printing, and Photography. Likewise, a helicopter outside a JATE hangar indicates the Establishment's

A visiting Tornado being refuelled at Brize Norton.

Above An Iraqi anti-aircraft gun captured by No.101 Squadron.

involvement in load-slinging equipment. It is a quiet corner of the airfield — apart from a nearby test bed for running up VC10 engines.

The perimeter road continues past JATE Headquarters and a large bay to the left where fire drills are held. The bay contains several aircraft hulks, some well scorched from real flames used in the drills. The main crash crews for RAF Brize Norton are located a little further along the road by the Air Traffic Control tower. The tower building houses Brize Radar which controls the surrounding air space, officially acknowledged as an 'Area of Intense Aerial Activity'. Apart from nearby aircraft movements, the location is again a quiet one. However, throughout every day and night of the year, Brize Radar is monitoring the surrounding skies.

The last set of buildings along the south-west side of the airfield comprises No.101 Squadron Headquarters. This is the Brize Squadron that specializes in air-to-air refuelling. This Squadron did notable RAF work with Vulcans in the 60s and 70s, then re-formed with converted VC10s in the mid-eighties. No.101 exploits are legendary, both in peace and war. Outside 101 Headquarters, stands some interesting weaponry.

'Iraqi anti-aircraft guns,' a 101 Squadron member remarks casually in passing.

Across the way, two VC10 K3s are being worked on by engineers. The aircraft interior and surrounds are strewn with pipes and hoses. Chapter 12 will describe how Brize people and aircraft turned air-to-air refuelling into an art.

After 101, the perimeter road turns once again towards the main runway, the western end this time. This time also, the traffic lights are at red as a Lockheed TriStar comes in to land. The large wide-bodied aircraft touches down like a feather then taxies past the waiting cars. A few moments later the lights are green again and ground traffic crosses the runway. The perimeter road curves towards the Station's quarters for single airmen and airwomen. Side roads lead to the previously mentioned Junior Ranks Restaurant, the swimming pool and Spotlight Club. The guided tour is over.

Yet only the surface has been touched. Much interesting work goes on behind the scenes, not least that done by Brize Norton's Engineering Wing. Not only is the Wing's work vital to keep aircraft flying, but the variety and extent of these technical duties also contain many surprises, as revealed in the following chapter.

Above right An operator on duty at Brize Radar.

Chapter 5

BASE HANGAR

The most visible part of RAF Brize Norton's Engineering Wing is Base Hangar. This structure dominates the north-eastern end of the Station and, amazingly, appears larger the moment one steps inside it. VC10s and TriStars are big planes, yet several can be housed with space to spare. The hangar was originally built to take six aircraft. On the day of the writer's initial visit, seven were present — albeit the last was half in and half outside. Wrapped entirely round the planes were mobile staging units with walkways, flights of steps and safety rails, rising to over 40 ft. RAF and civilian engineers were everywhere — high on the work platforms, inside fuselages and wings, engine nacelles and undercarriage bays, on the hangar floor and in nearby workshops. Among these technicians some keep regular hours, others are on shifts and there are teams continuing round the clock. In addition to those responsible for aircraft maintenance, there are also those maintaining the vast hangar itself. It is truly a non-stop place.

Even so, Base Hangar is only part of the Engineering Wing's many activities. A start has been made here because it houses the core task — that of keeping Brize planes flying. Unlike RAF Lyneham, where four Squadrons share a fleet of 60 Hercules, the three Brize Squadrons fly their own aircraft as follows:

No.10 Squadron has 13 VC10 CMK1 passenger/freight aircraft which are currently being converted, as will be described.

A rare sight of the 1045 ft-long Base Hangar without aircraft in front of it.

No.101 Squadron operates nine VC10 K2 and K3 tanker versions with five K4s on the way.

As for the third Brize Squadron, No.216, it flies eight TriStars designated C2, K1 and KC1. C2 is passenger only, K1 is also for passengers but has air-to-air refuelling capability, while KC1 will take passengers, cargo and can be refuelled in flight.

Regarding No.10 Squadron's 13 VC10 CMK1s, eight are presently under conversion by British Aerospace in conjunction with flight refuelling at Hurn Airport, Bournemouth. The addition of underwing pods will make then into VC10 CMK1(K)s. There is an option for a further five and, if all 13 are converted, the programme will continue until 1994. With regard to No.101 Squadron's addition of five K4s, these will be civil Super VC10 aircraft that once belonged to British Airways. The five are being converted by British Aerospace at its Filton, Bristol, factory. RAF Brize Norton expects to receive the first VC10 K4 in late 1992, with subsequent aircraft arriving at the rate of one every three months.

The rolling programmes outlined above show the formidable workload confronting Engineering Wing at Brize Norton. Yet the task is but one of many. A complex situation may best be explained by first outlining recent policy changes, then the organization of the Wing itself.

The technical support of Brize-based aircraft was radically adapted for the 1990s. The Station's Engineering Wing used to include Line Servicing Squadron (LSS) which did First Line work for all aircraft on the Station. The Wing also carried out maintenance and overhauls. In 1990 First Line Servicing was transferred to No.10 Squadron. Like No.101 Squadron, it now has its own Engineering Flight. In the case of No.216 Squadron's TriStars, these were originally maintained by a combination of RAF and civilian engineers, but the Engineering Flight is solely staffed by RAF technicians.

Another change for the 90s was that overhauls were transferred from Strike Command, in which RAF Brize Norton is included, to nearby RAF Abingdon of Support Command. The same work is still done in Brize's Base Hangar, but by No.3 Aircraft Maintenance Squadron (No.3 AMS) which reports to Abingdon. That is not all. In addition to having Brize and Abingdon RAF personnel, the Base Hangar contains contingents from British Aerospace, Rolls Royce and other civilian companies.

So much for recent organizational changes. The Engineering Wing at RAF Brize

Five aircraft associated with Brize Norton. (Left to right) Comet, Hercules, Britannia, VC10 and Belfast.

Norton can only be understood, and the diversity of its work be fully appreciated, by examining the component parts. After all, it is the largest of its kind in the Royal Air Force. Briefly, to begin with, the Wing has five Squadrons, each made up of two or more flights. As already stated, it serves the Station's three flying Squadrons. It also gives technical advice to many others and (what is called) 'parents' a lot more.

Starting with the five Squadrons, they are:

Engineering Operations Squadron (EOS)

Aircraft Engineering Squadron (AES)

Electrical Engineering Squadron (EES)

Mechanical Transport Squadron (MTS)

Mechanical Engineering Ground Squadron (MEGS)

Engineering Operations Squadron

EOS is essentially the headquarters Squadron for the whole Engineering Wing. As such it is located in the Passenger Terminal building near to the Operations Room and the Station Commander's office. A representative from Engineering is always on duty in the Operations Room, which itself never closes, and the Engineering Wing Commander is among the first to be called by the Station Commander when major demands are made on RAF Brize Norton.

The three main tasks of the Engineering Operations Squadron are to provide maintenance planning control of the Wing, to co-ordinate ground support of flying operations and to assist with all technical aspects of Station life. It also administers the VC10 and TriStar Ground Maintenance School, thereby ensuring that engineering training appropriate to each aircraft type is provided to all Station engineers. Last but not least, Station Publications and Forms Sections (SPFS) provides the necessary technical documentation which record the life history of each aircraft. This history is essential for the control of airworthiness activities, and to ensure the reliability of the aircraft.

A quick meeting finishes and members depart to their Units. Outside windows — muted also by well engineered glazing — are VC10s, TriStars, a visiting Hercules. Passengers file out to their aircraft. Freight is being loaded into holds. Large bowsers refuel. Whenever a plane takes off it represents the culmination of engineering efforts, often over many weeks.

Aircraft Engineering Squadron

AES, mainly located in Base Hangar, is responsible for Second Line maintenance of VC10 CMK1 and K2 and K3 aircraft. Two flights address themselves to this main task. Work on the aircraft is carried out by Scheduled Maintenance Flight (SMF), and work on its components, removed to nearby bays, is done by Aircraft Engineering Support Flight (AESF).

SMF consists of some 60 technical tradesmen under the command of a flight lieutenant and his Senior NCOs. His and their world revolves round Bays 1-4 in the Base Hangar. Apart from scheduled work, a host of engineering problems — like the proverbial buck — are passed to them. Fuel leaks, hydraulic pressure down, flying controls sloppy — the aircraft with the complaint goes to SMF. Their technicians have to identify and rectify while working, in most instances, under pressure. Theirs is a tough calling.

In the case of Aircraft Engineering Support Flight (AESF) its 70 members are concerned with a range of airframe, engine and ancillary equipment. Their activities

The range of ground equipment needed to service one VC10.

are carried out in the bays and workshops at the back of the Base Hangar close to the aircraft in for maintenance and repair. There is a Structures Bay for airframe-related work, an Engine Bay for VC10 Conways and TriStar RB211s, also a Pod Bay to deal with air-to-air refuelling equipment. The Flight includes a workforce for painting and finishing. The smart appearance of Brize aircraft is a tribute to their efforts.

It has to be repeated that RAF Brize Norton's Base Hangar, so impressive from the outside and inside, is in reality a place for solving problems. To begin with there are

Inside Base Hangar. A VC10 tanker in foreground and a VC10 passenger transport behind it.

Typical view inside Base Hangar showing scaffolding and maintenance equipment round a VC10.

different RAF Units working together. Add to these the civilian contingents from several outside firms and it will be understood that a substantial slice of diplomacy is required in every person's mental make-up. Fortunately all are engineers with a common built-in discipline. Nevil Shute, the aeronautical engineer-cum-writer, summed up such situations when he said: 'The engineer can't cheat or the bridge will fall down.' This attitude is most applicable to aircraft, especially those providing air bridges around the world — as Brize ones do.

'Not going anywhere at the moment,' said the RAF engineer.

Moving on to technical problems, it is often said — perhaps too readily — that the RAF has a splendid tradition of taking over old aircraft and keeping them flying. The de Havilland Comet, following its early troubles, and the Bristol Britannia, after its civilian life, are but two examples. In the case of the VC10, originally designed and manufactured by Vickers to first flight in 1962, its airways role was intended to last 15 years. In 1966 the RAF acquired 14 VC10 CMK1s from what was then BOAC, and in 1984 nine from East African Airways. Today, Brize is still flying VC10s and, more to the point, successfully maintaining them. Five more aircraft are due to come on stream in the mid-1990s.

Which is all very well. The buck previously mentioned as being passed to Engineering Wing comes to its final stop in Base Hangar. The engineers there talk openly and precisely about structural and repair work required to keep the VC10s flying. Technical people, Service and civilians alike, have to meet these problems head on. They cannot duck them, yet this may lead to personal problems. A huge effort like the Gulf War — getting men and equipment out there, then back again — required immense efforts on everyone's part. A well-earned respite over the summer then allowed all the engineers to return to the normal pressures of air transportation maintenance.

To conclude this brief attempt to summarize the work done and problems solved by AES personnel in Base Hangar, mention should be made of its Computer Services. The system (PRIME) was installed as an aid to management in the planning and progressing of aircraft maintenance work. Terminals sited throughout the hangar are used by engineers working there to obtain all kinds of information, such as spares availability from the central control room. The system also incorporates computer-aided design and printing facilities to reproduce maintenance programmes, repair schemes, dimensional drawings and organization charts.

On the subject of design, the amazing and interesting structure of the Base Hangar at RAF Brize Norton will be covered later in this Chapter. Meanwhile, here is the third and no less important Squadron of the Station's Engineering Wing.

Electrical Engineering Squadron

Somehow the word 'electrical' in the title seems a bit of a misnomer reminiscent of old aero engines with magnetos linked to hefty brass on-off switches in open cockpits. On the other hand, the present state of electrical art as applied to aviation covers avionics, communication and information technology. This is the area in which EES operates.

The Electrical Engineering Squadron at Brize Norton occupies a prime south-facing site by the airfield. It is conveniently close to aircraft on the 10 Squadron pan and the Base Hangar. Its workshops are well lit, air-conditioned and spotlessly clean as is necessary when dealing with electronic equipment. The task of EES at Brize is to provide Second Line support for VC10 and some TriStar avionics. It also looks after a comprehensive range of ground navigation and communication equipment, the Station's flight simulators, and provides photographic support to the Station. The advanced synthetic trainers (ASTs) are used for VC10 C and K flight simulation, while pilots training on TriStars use an AST at London Airport.

Much of what Electrical Engineering Squadron does is highly technical and, by its very nature, security restricted. To the visitor, EES work seems to consist of dealing with black boxes, each more intricate than the last. But there is one understandable activity gathering pace at Brize Norton — that of improving communication on the Station. The first phase is named SAMA for Station Administrative Management Aid. This will enable servicemen and women to obtain information which, in the past, either required a phone call or walking to their nearest Personnel Documentation (PD) point. Instead there will be 70 terminals located around the

Work in a VC10 electric bay under the main cabin floor.

Station, 50 of them within Personnel Management headquarters to answer all queries. These terminals are all linked in a large network by a powerful mainframe computer.

The second phase is for RAF Brize Norton to install and run its own telephone system. For a start this will involve laying over 30 miles of new cable ducting. In the end, however, the new system will mean that every key person on the base will have his or her personal telephone. Moreover, holders will be able to programme their Units to redirect calls or recall numbers that are engaged. A third phase will involve special electronic equipment to ensure privacy of voice and data transmissions. All this EES work, which was started before, then postponed by the Gulf War, is scheduled for completion in 1993. It will save time as well as increase efficiency throughout the air base.

Mechanical Transport Squadron

Here again the word 'mechanical', like that of 'electrical', could be regarded as another misnomer. MT to most means Motor Transport, though much mechanical hardware is handled by this Squadron. Whichever way one looks at it, the curious fact is so many people take MT for granted. Necessary, they may admit, while the reality is that without Mechanical (or Motor) Transport a Station — especially a large air base like Brize — would simply seize up. MTS at Brize has 420 vehicles of its own, to maintain, plus a further 300 or more at various Units around the Station. Maintenance Flight also provides painting facilities for all these vehicles.

The MT Squadron at Brize has some 188 Service Personnel made up of 140 drivers and 43 technicians, electricians and painter/finishers in two flights called Operations and Maintenance. As the flight names indicate, MT Ops plans, allocates and moves vehicles while MT Maintenance keeps them running. In addition there are about 50 civilian drivers on call for the many and varied tasks confronting the Squadron.

What do they all do? Their main tasks are concerned with providing transport and special vehicle support for the Flying and Training Squadrons as well as the Engineering and Supply Wings. They similarly serve other Units such as Brize Radar, the Tactical Communications Wing, JATE and the RAF Regiment. Loads are constantly on the move round the Station, between Brize and Lyneham, and elsewhere. The ferrying of service passengers between the Station, civil airports and other Service Units is another massive and never-ending task.

One of the MT Squadron's major assignments is to support the Parachute Training

A VC10 forward freight bay.

Below right Internal inspection. A never-ending task for Brize Norton engineers.

Below Removing a VC10 brake Unit.

School. There are drops all over the country which require Brize coaches and ambulances. Five coaches are needed for an average drop and two stand-by ambulances which in turn require medical staff. In addition, a truck and further

Two Base Hangar Senior NCO engineers assess panel repair.

personnel are required to collect the parachutes for subsequent checking and repacking. The whole exercise depends on transport support.

Another problem facing the already complex duties of the MT Squadron is that of detachments. Personnel and vehicles are apt to disappear overseas to remote regions needing tractors, bowsers and aircraft loaders. During Operation Granby, many aircraft — including old RAF Belfasts and the Russian Antonov 124 — were co-opted for moving MT equipment to the Gulf. As for personnel movements, MT people are a special breed taking all that is thrown at them and coming back for more. One driver from another Station, which shall be nameless, came into Brize requesting more cash. He had been on the road for two months due to being given another load wherever he went.

Mechanical Engineering Ground Squadron

Last but not least in this list of the five Squadrons that make up the Engineering Wing is what everyone refers to as MEGS. Personnel and location-wise, this Squadron is a large one and widely spread around the Station. In fact it has four flights, and works at 13 sites. These are Visiting Aircraft and Role Equipment, Ground Equipment Servicing, and Airframe Components and Armanents. MEGS also has additional specialist sections dealing with survival gear such as escape chutes life rafts and non-destructive testing. The NDT team serves aircraft throughout southern England and supports REME operations in 28 locations around the world. As an MEGS man put it: 'We keep fairly busy.'

Regarding the Visiting Aircraft and Role Equipment Flight, most of its fascinating

Washing down a VC10 outside Base Hangar.

work will be covered in Chapter 10 which is devoted to the preparation of aircraft for VIP usage. Suffice it to say here that this flight looks after all visiting aircraft and maintains everything necessary for important travellers. The work involves stripping aircraft to basic frames, then fitting new bulkheads and doors as necessary. The process continues with wall panels, curtains and carpets, seats and other furnishings down to headrest covers, pillows and blankets. Every single item is present and perfect.

The Ground Equipment Servicing Flight of MEGS is responsible for items such as passenger steps and freight lifters, ground power units, aircraft towbars and hydraulic rigs. Armament Flight sees to the storage of weapons and explosives, a task which increased by quantum leaps during the Gulf conflict.

The Airframe Components Flight maintains a series of workshops and bays for the handling and testing of aircraft parts, materials and systems. On the hydraulics side there are the Skydrol and OM15 bays. Nearby are the undercarriage and tyre areas. A fridge bay takes care of aircraft refrigerators and air-conditioning units. There is an

Final preparation of a VC10.

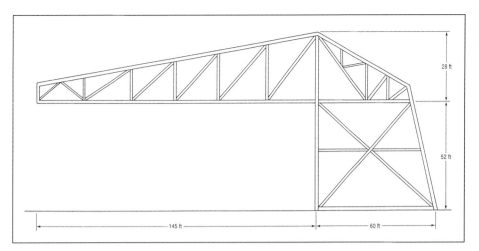

Figure 1. The main cantilever frame of Base Hangar.

28 ft

52 ft

145 ft

60 ft

oxygen bay for use both on aircraft systems and for parachute work. Another ACF specialist job is the repair of reinforced plastic components.

Base Hangar

Brize Norton's Base Hangar is such a prominent feature of the place that more should be told about its unique design and construction. Most people only see the back where there are car parks and various buildings such as the boiler house. From that side the roof looks odd, with disproportionate sections sticking into the skyline. The way to view Base Hangar is from the airfield or the apron immediately in front of it, and then the true nature of this impressive structure is revealed.

Doors 50 ft high run the entire 1045 ft length of the hangar and, if necessary, all can be opened to provide uninterrupted entry or exit to the interior from end to end. In other words there are no pillars along the entire front. The vast roof, with its lights, cranes and other services, seems to stay up there as if by magic. Of course, everything

Wing Commander Hill, former OC Engineering Wing, showing Lord Ironside round Base Hangar.

Bill Godwin, who was a fitter at Brize Norton from 1941-45, returns to see present-day work in Base Hangar.

stays up there, not by magic, but by fine civil engineering. Figure 1, Main cantilever frame of Base Hangar, shows how it was done. It also explains why, when Base Hangar is viewed from the back, there are those odd angles sticking into the air.

When this hangar for RAF Brize Norton was wanted in the mid-60s the basic requirement put to its designers was that six large transport aircraft should be able to enter, fit comfortably and have the one door shut behind them. The structure, therefore, had to be spacious and not incorporate hard protrusions for the tender wingtips of aircraft to touch. The lightest such contact would put a plane out of service for weeks if not months. It is interesting to record that the designers of Brize's Base Hangar looked at 14 single, double and other cantilever structures around the world.

1950	Partial Cantilever	Copenhagen, Denmark
1956	Single Cantilever	Philadelphia, USA
1957	Double Cantilever	Kansas City, USA
1958	Double Cantilever	Miami, USA
1959	Single Cantilever	Orly, France
1959	Semi Cantilever	Chateauroux, France
1960	Single Cantilever	Rome, Italy
1960	Double Cantilever	Los Angeles, USA
1960	Double Cantilever	Idlewild, USA
1960	Double Cantilever	San Francisco, USA
1960	Double Cantilever	Frankfurt, German
1963	Single Cantilever	Rome, Italy
1965	Single Cantiever	Gatwick, UK
1966	Single Cantilever	Ballykelly, UK

The above list is a simplification as some of the hangars were built with pre-stressed concrete, while others used steel frames and cladding. Brize's Base Hangar followed the latter course like the last two built in the UK.

Half of the TriStar tail dock. The dock is internally fitted with steps and working platforms.

RAF Brize Norton's Base Hangar was commissioned by the Ministry of Defence and designed by the Ministry of Public Buildings. The erection of the steel structure and its fabrication was begun in February 1966 and completed in February 1967. The

Figure 2. Plan view of Base Hangar.

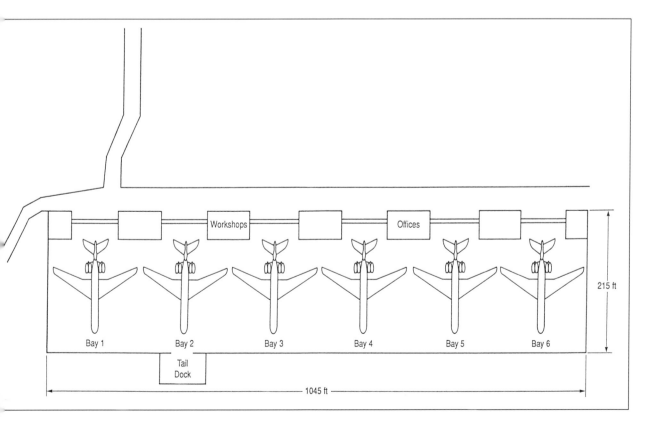

largest structural members delivered to the site were 88 ft long and weighed 22 tons. Each main frame weighs 99 tons and, in total, 3000 tons of steel were used in the construction. After finishing, the hangar was formally handed over to the Royal Air Force on 16 August 1967. It has been in continuous use ever since.

Figure 2, Plan view of Base Hangar, shows it with six VC10s in situ. Built around the bases of the cantilever frames along the back wall are engineering offices, stores and workshops with more work bays between them. It will be seen that the VC10s are brought in tail first and the design allows generous space for the high tailplane. The protrusion, called the 'Tail Dock', in front of Bay 2 was added later to take a TriStar which enters the hangar nose first. The Tail Dock is fitted internally with steps and working platforms so that, when this aircraft is in dock, engineers can reach the full height of its tall tail.

The hangar design allows much needed space around all aircraft positions for movable staging, servicing equipment, towing tractors and fork-lift trucks. The clearance factor for tail-planes is $10\frac{1}{2}$ ft from any obstruction and that between wing tips of adjacent aircraft is $12\frac{1}{2}$ ft.

In order to handle the engines and other large components, electrically-operated travelling cranes, capable of lifting one and five tons, are installed in the roof. Electricity and compressed air are housed in floor pits sited to serve each of the six aircraft positions in their respective bays. The maintenance task requires a high level of lighting whatever the weather, and overhead lamps give an illumination of 15 lumens/ft2 which can be augmented by use of wander lamps. Heaters for the hangar interior — and for deterring a build-up of snow on the roof - are provided to give a working temperature of 60oF. However, as with most hangars, this is hard to maintain and during the cold Cotswold winters the system is supplemented by space heaters. Precautions against fire are comprehensive and stringent, the priorities being to personnel, aircraft and the building in that order.

Aviation engineers know that all aircraft, especially those in a hangar, constitute a definite fire hazard. So smoking is strictly forbidden, as is footwear with metal tips. There are constant lectures and fire drills so that newcomers to the Base Hangar are well aware of the right procedures in any emergency. Working with high voltage electrical equipment is another hazard about which all personnel are instructed. Other potential dangers abound because the entire place, of necessity, contains multiple cable runs and air lines, overhead cranes and staging from which objects may

Resident and visiting aircraft outside Base Hangar.

trip, protrude, swing or fall. Added to these are sudden distracting noises from pneumatic power tools and riveting guns. The Base Hangar at RAF Brize Norton is really a place for the experienced and the careful.

Further caution is needed with the hangar doors. These represent an important part of the structure and, at 10% of the building's value, a considerable cost item — like £5 million. So trucks and aircraft are always kept well clear. The doors themselves are of the sliding/folding type. While everything can be pulled right back, the individual doors are so arranged that access can be gained to each aircraft bay without the others being opened. The folding leaves are supported by upright hinges. The tops of these uprights run in door head slots and are supported in floor rails. Actuation is by eight $7\frac{1}{2}$ hp electric motors through a system of winches and cables. Door speed is brisk (100ft a minute) controlled by push buttons. There are limit switches to prevent over-bunching or over-extension. The leaf panels are of aluminium, for lightness, sandwiching thermal insulation. Twelve self-closing wicket doors are incorporated to allow quick access to and from the outside apron.

Other Engineering Wing Activities

It has been mentioned that, apart from the Wing's prime tasks carried out by its five engineering Squadrons, there are many other allied activities. These include helping the three flying Squadrons and the Operational Conversion Unit, as well as assisting all other Station Units, the RAF Regiment and the Flying Club.

'Parenting' was also mentioned. Should this be regarded as an afterthought, non-Service readers might be interested to know what it means. Like every RAF Unit, the Engineering Wing at Brize Norton works to clear-cut instructions on its tasks, duties and responsibilities. These continue for page after page, then right at the end comes Annex A — Parenting. This Annex adds another 55 tasks, a wide spectrum of technical areas where the Wing has to respond and help if asked — which it invariably does.

First come the UK places and the services to be made available. There is the care of ground equipment at RAF Innsworth for example. RAF Benson in one direction has its liquid oxygen work done by Brize engineers who also see to 'all necessary services' at RAF Weston-on-the-Green. An embracing term, 'all necessary services.' Looking down the list it occurs at RAF Fairford and RAF Little Rissington. Well, these are not too far away. A pleasant drive over the Cotswolds. Then the next two items land like a double punch. RAF Belize — general engineering services, and Dakar — ground equipment. The list goes on to cover Calgary — all services, Bahrain, Colombo and somewhere known as Sek Kong.

And still there is more. Many of the places hold several responsibilities for the Engineering Wing at Brize Norton. A typical grouping is as follows:

Defence weaponry
Explosive storage
Mechanical transport
Parachute equipment
Provision of transport
Signals traffic
Technical administration

The responsibility for the above is difficult enough on one's home ground, but quite another matter half way round the world. It is to be hoped that the surface coverage, which is all this chapter can give, will help others to understand the task of RAF Brize Norton's Engineering Wing.

Chapter 6

ACTIVE AIRCRAFT

The British Aerospace VC10s and the Lockheed TriStar are not exactly new aircraft. Both saw years of civil airline service before reaching the RAF. Yet, owing to some inspired adaptation and dedicated usage, supported by superb engineering, these planes have taken on new lives. They are certainly very active aircraft.

Starting with the VC10 CMK1, as operated by No.10 Squadron, here are a few facts and figures. It is 158 ft in length, has a height of 40 ft, its wing span is 146 ft and tail span 44 ft. Powered by four Rolls Royce Conway 301 engines, each developing 22,500 lb thrust, the VC10 has a cruising speed of 550 mph up to 43,000 ft. Its maximum take-off weight is 323,000 lb, max. landing weight 235,000 lb and typical landing speed 140 mph. The thirteen VC10 C MK1s of No.10 Squadron differ in several important areas from VC10 Standards and Supers. The CMK1 is a hybrid which combined the shorter and lighter fuselage of the Standard with the higher thrust engines and more efficient wings of the Super. The cabin floor has been substantially strengthened to take high density loads and a large freight door fitted on the port side of the aircraft.

The VC10 C MK1s of No.10 Squadron at Brize operate in three main roles — passenger, freight or a combination of both. A maximum of 141 passengers plus crew can be carried or, in a matter or hours, all passenger seats can be removed and 22 tons of freight loaded. The nominal range is around 4000 miles, but this can be extended almost indefinitely by air-to-air refuelling. All the VC10s at Brize Norton, as do most of the aircraft on the Station strength, have refuelling probes so as to receive fuel in flight. Some of the amazing feats made possible by AAF techniques will be described in this and other chapters.

A walk round and through the VC10 clearly shows that it is a good solid aircraft. It stands, one might say, three square on hefty undercarriage legs, and the rudder fin towers up to the flying tailplane actuated by its own electric motor and gearbox system. An auxiliary power unit is housed in the rear end of the fuselage. This small turbine engine generates the aircraft's own electrical and pneumatic power for ground use, thus giving the VC10 valuable flexibility as a military transport.

Inside, the RAF VC10s differ from present-day civil airliners in two noticeable aspects. First, it has a four-man flight deck of two pilots, a navigator and an air engineer. Secondly, in the passenger cabin, all the seats face rearwards. Passengers are looked after by an Air Loadmaster who is assisted, depending on the aircraft's role, by up to three stewards. The cabin can also be converted to take a maximum of 60 stretcher cases.

No.10 Squadron, situated close to the Passenger Terminal, provides air transport for Service personnel and freight, and also for VIPs. There are six main types of flight.

Proportions differ from year to year, but the following are typical — Exercises 50%, Schedules 23%, Specials 12%, Routes, Operations and VIPs 5% each. Exercise tasks are to tri-Service requirements, as co-ordinated by the Ministry of Defence, and vary from month to month. These may include taking Royal Engineers to Africa, an Armoured Brigade to Canada or Gurkhas to and from the Far East. Scheduled flights are to regular destinations such as Washington, Belize or Cyprus. Many of these are planned up to a year in advance.

Specials include aeromedical work, such as responding to an international relief effort, also the carrying of diplomatic mail and logistic equipment. Route work covers both local and distant crew training. New crews have to acquire practical experience, and that is achieved by flying with veteran crews around the UK, Europe and North America. At the same time the aircraft is used for other tasks such as picking up and delivering loads. Regarding Operations, one of these can suddenly escalate, as during the Falklands and Gulf campaigns.

While the VIP flights are a small proportion of No.10 Squadron's programme, they do demand a great deal of work. Everyone the writer met was proud and honoured to carry out these duties for senior officers and officials, Cabinet ministers, the Prime Minister and the Royal Family.

Understandably only the best crews are selected — those with long service and a high level of experience. Apart from the meticulous fitting out and checking of the entire aircraft, the crews for VIP work set themselves further disciplines and standards. For example, if the VIP passenger is due to arrive at 10.36 hrs, No.10 Squadron will try to do this — to the second. They will plan their whole flight, make allowances for air traffic on the way as well as during approach, touchdown and taxiing, so as to line up the VIP exit door with the end of the red carpet at 10.36 hrs exactly.

Turning now to No.10 Squadron, this is made up of around 200 aircrew members comprising captains, co-pilots, navigators, air engineers, Loadmasters and stewards, plus ground crews. In the Squadron's Operations Room a simple system of name tags on a desk board shows where every person is. Wall charts also indicate aircraft movements for the present month, together with those of last month and planning for next month. These easy-to-read visual displays are backed by many forms of information technology. Telephones keep ringing, telexes and faxes chatter out messages, computer screens ripple to table the next batch of data. A typical question is entered. The computer is asked what other planes will be in the air when a Brize VC10 flies over the Atlantic to Washington tomorrow? Back comes an instant answer detailing all other aircraft, their routes, times and speeds.

The Squadron's Operations Room is flanked by offices for crew members — pilots, navigators, engineers, Loadmasters and stewards. Two names were chosen at random from different wall charts to learn their lifestyles over a month. The results were typical, not only of No.10 Squadron work, but also of present-day RAF activities.

In the case of the pilot, he began his month with three days in Washington followed by two days off. Next, because he is a keen runner, the pilot was due to compete in a marathon, after which he was off again to the States for a week. On his return there was another road race before he made two flights across Europe. Finally, he would end his month in Washington.

The navigator would begin his month crewing an RAF yacht at Cowes. He would then return to join a standby crew and man the office over a weekend. This would be followed by six days flying to and around Canada, after which he had two days rest before proving himself on a series of flight simulation tests. Another day of stand-by was followed by a week in the office, then back to Canada.

However, as one pilot of No.10 Squadron expressed it, the main task of the RAF is to prepare for war. When the Gulf Crisis begin to erupt during the Summer of 1990, the Squadron doubled, then more than trebled its normal flying hours. Passenger,

A VC10 tanker on the
runway at Ascension
Island.

freight and training programmes combined would average 400 hrs a month. From August 1990 to April 1991 this monthly figure rose dramatically to 700, 900, 1200 and, at peak periods, to over 1400 flying hours. Much has been said of Lyneham's Hercules taking men and materials to the Gulf. It was all a magnificent effort, the No.10 Squadron pilot agreed, but our VC10s took twice as much twice as fast. We often went there and back in a day.

While No.10 Squadron's VC10s were meeting all troop and weapon carrying demands, they maintained their scheduled flights to Europe, the Mediterranean, North and Central America. In addition the Squadron fitted in every VIP demand made on it. For example, the Prime Minister had to make a three-day visit to the theatre of war and allied countries (London—Riyadh—Jubayl—Dhahran—Muscat—Cairo—London). On top of that there was considerable ministerial, diplomatic and military staff activity with VIPs criss-crossing the Middle East.

During this hectic period, when No.10 Squadron's aircraft were more likely to be flying than on the ground, their reliability proved to be excellent. To give but one idea of the loads they shifted: a Tornado can carry four 1000 lb bombs. The VC10 moved these to the Gulf 50 at a time. For the record, the 350 men and women of No.10 Squadron contributed 1326 sorties and over 5000 extra hours in support of British forces during the campaign. And, as will be seen, No.101 Squadron's VC10 tanker versions made an equally impressive contribution.

It was mentioned in the last chapter that No.101 Squadron currently operates nine

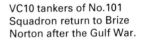
VC10 tankers of No.101 Squadron return to Brize Norton after the Gulf War.

Passengers board a VC10 CMk1 at Brize.

Below A receiver pilot's view of a VC10 tanker during air refuelling.

VC10 K2 and K3 tankers. It was also mentioned at the beginning of this chapter how the Standard VC10 (shorter, lighter) differs from the Super (higher thrust engines and more efficient wings). The K2 and K3 tanker versions are Standards and Supers respectively. Their vital statistics are much the same as those of the CMK1s apart from ingenious air-to-air refuelling installations.

Each VC10 tanker aircraft has three refuelling points — one in a specially constructed bay under the rear fuselage, and the other two in pods below the main outer wings. This arrangement enables a large transport/tanker/surveillance aircraft to be refuelled from the rear fuselage unit or two combat aircraft to receive fuel simultaneously from the wing pods. The underbay unit has a transfer rate of 500 gal/min and each wing pod delivers at 300 gal/min.

The VC10s carry their own fuel in various wing tanks, and there is an extra tail tank in the case of the Supers. Further fuel for the K2/K3s is accommodated in five large cylindrical tanks in what was the passenger cabin. Tanker aircraft can also receive fuel via the 9 ft long nose-mounted probe just above the radome. The system which includes night lights and television cameras, works in even the most exacting circumstances, as will now be revealed.

Early in August 1990 the worsening Iraq/Kuwait situation became the Operation Granby build-up which escalated to the Operation Desert Storm Gulf War in mid-January 1991. Personnel of No.101 Squadron, enjoying the summer days at their pleasant site on the far side of Brize airfield reflected that they might be required . . . sometime. Within a week everyone had been recalled from leave and the Squadron was in the thick of it. The opening operation involved helping ten Tornados reach Cyprus by refuelling them over Sicily. All too soon, No.101 Squadron tankers were strung out along routes from the UK right down to the Gulf helping Tornados, Jaguars and other aircraft get there. Accommodation during this period varied from air-conditioned sea front hotels to desert tents in 130°F of heat.

Below right Refuelling a VC10.

From that August until November, No.101 Squadron tankers were working in twos and threes, either on routine operations or developing refuelling tactics to suit desert conditions. The latter meant low level flying and learning the hard way about sandstorms and thunderstorms, to name but two hazards. Temperatures remained over 100°F, but everyone soon became acclimatized. By then there were so many aircraft around that one Squadron humorist described his airport as being covered by wall-to-wall aeroplanes. In addition to combat and tanker aircraft, there were transports of ever-increasing sizes; also the US Navy, Air Force and Marines carrier-based fighters and bombers kept dropping in from time to time whether or not there was room.

In mid-December 1990, all nine tanker aircraft of No.101 Squadron moved from various airfield deployments to Riyadh. This fine airport is some 300 miles from the Gulf coast at the upland centre and capital of Saudi Arabia. Logistically and communications-wise the move made life a little easier for the Squadron's 50 air crew and about 100 ground personnel. Everyone remained healthy and all aircraft stayed serviceable. In fact, No.101 was the only RAF Squadron deployed en masse from its home base. While there was not a single health or compassionate case, the Squadron managed to keep rotating crews back to Brize in one aircraft at a time for short breaks and maintenance checks. About half the Squadron managed to see their homes and families, either before or at Christmas. Those who remained at Riyadh say they were inundated by plum puddings.

In mid-January 1991, Operation Granby switched to Desert Storm. Suddenly all those hours spent in Brize lecture rooms and in flight simulators, followed by repeated exercises, proved their worth. The general public in Britain and the rest of the world marvelled at the television coverage of combat aircraft taking off on allotted missions. Only occasionally would a commentator mention air-to-air refuelling, but few know exactly what that entailed. For those at home it is hard to imagine, let alone credit, the techniques flawlessly carried out night after night.

Think of 24 Tornados taking off from their airfield by the coast. They are laden with armaments, so the less fuel initially carried during take-off and climb the better. At about the same time 300 miles away, five VC10 tankers of 101 Squadron became airborne, each with over 80 tons of fuel aboard. The Tornados and VC10s converge, then meet. In pairs, the Tornados take on four tons of fuel apiece while on their way towards Iraq. Just before reaching that country, the Tornados top up with another two tons apiece, then cross over into enemy territory.

Meanwhile, the five tankers, just inside the Saudi border, are flying round and round what their crews come to call the racetrack. This they do for 1½ hours until the Tornados return. At last the combat aircraft are reunited with their respective tankers. They fill up once more before peeling away towards their coastal base. When all the thirsty Tornados have been satisfied, the five tankers head for Riyadh. For that operation alone, there have been 72 link-ups performed in complete radio silence and in the darkness of the desert night.

Similar operations were carried out by No.101 Squadron's nine tankers night after night. Later, as the enemy air threat lessened, the Tornados flew at higher levels and refuelling link-ups rose from 1000 to over 30,000 feet. At least 90% of all RAF attack sorties were dependent on air-to-air refuelling. Close to 3000 receiving aircraft were refuelled during hostilities alone, of which a quarter were aircraft from other allied forces. It was not uncommon to refuel aircraft of three or four nations concurrently and, on one occasion, a VC10 tanker supported British, French, Canadian and Saudi receivers while being controlled by an American AWACS aircraft.

The fame of No.101 Squadron tankers spread, especially among the US forces. Life became busier and more interesting refuelling Hornets, Tomcats, Intruders and Corsairs. As one Squadron member recalled, it also became a life of 'fly, sleep, eat and fly.' And, he added, 'there were Scud alerts just as one fell asleep'. By the end of January 1991, the nine tankers had been on 106 missions in 15 days, making it 180 for that month, followed by 279 in February. They flew near 400 war missions which, combined with the Operation Granby build-up came to a grand total in excess of 3000 sorties. One more total — the amount of fuel transferred was 5.7 million gallons!

Following the cease fire, everyone wanted to go home. However, for 101 Squadron it was not that easy. Together with other tanker aircraft, making 100 in all, the Squadron helped Tornados, Jaguars, Buccaneers, transports, et al to Cyprus, Italy, Germany and finally back to RAF Brize Norton. On 13 March four aircraft flew in together, followed by the remaining five in quick succession after seven months in the Gulf. Their nine tanker aircraft landed and taxied with precision towards the pan behind a heavily laden Guinness lorry. Someone, who should be promoted ever upwards, reckoned it would be appreciated after their efforts in a 'dry' country.

Summing up, the VC10s of Nos.10 and 101 Squadrons did all that was required of them. If aircraft have human characteristic — and most airmen will swear they do — then these were certainly active. However, to be less fanciful, it really comes down to training. The primary aim of No.241 Operational Conversion Unit at RAF Brize Norton is to train aircrews on both variants of the VC10, the CMK1 transports and the K tankers. The Unit is structured in three flights — namely, Air Transport, Air-to-Air Refuelling and Simulators. The AAR Flight runs a school to teach everyone in the RAF involved with flight refuelling.

Air Transport Flight is responsible for converting both new and experienced pilots to the VC10 CMK1, the course lasting five months. It also runs refresher courses applicable to No.10 Squadron because, as with all pilots, navigators, air engineers and the rest, they must maintain peak proficiency. Regular check-ups are therefore made half-yearly and these can take up to a fortnight depending on experience. Standards are kept high by relentless training and ruthless examinations. Even the OCU instructors, who are the cream of the cream, are checked themselves by other

RAF and media greeting No.101 Squadron back from the Gulf War.

examiners from No.1 Group. It is not a system for 'just getting by'.

The Air-to-Air Refuelling Flight is run by 12 aircrew instructors. These AAR specialists are made up of pilots, navigators and air engineers. They are responsible for a variety of flight refuelling courses starting with conversion to VC10 tankers. There are also courses when a tanker co-pilot seeks upgrading to that of captain, and those needing to have skills on both VC10 variants — i.e. passenger and tanker. For example, No.10 Squadron engaged on air transport has a proportion of pilots available for tanker duties. There are further courses for Station executives wishing to have wide-ranging abilities in order to appreciate and help those more closely concerned.

Every aircrew member — captains, co-pilots, navigators and air engineers — has to undergo regular and intensive sessions on Brize's two flight simulators. Every month. The Station's simulator building, close by No.241 OCU, is surrounded by lawns and trees. These make it look a peaceful place until one steps inside. Once through the front doors, there is no doubt as to how busy everyone is. Aircrew personnel, instructors and simulator staff are all on the go from early morning until late at night to meet flying and training programmes.

The flight simulators were designed to operate 20 hours a day, and at RAF Brize Norton they more often than not do that. Simulators are now well known for their worth, also what they look like. Nevertheless, the sight of one in action is always impressive — a full size mock-up of an aircraft nose section held aloft on a platform that is precisely moved by six hydraulically-operated legs. Fitted over the flight deck window is an ingenious triple projector system optically arranged to give the captain and co-pilot 140º of vision. The scenes thus projected, those of airfields around the world, are depicted at the most difficult period, that of dusk. Rain and snow; high winds, pressure and temperature changes can all be simulated.

At RAF Brize Norton, the two flight simulators — one for VC10 C MK1 air

Below left A VC10 navigator's control panel.

Below A VC10 air engineer's control panel.

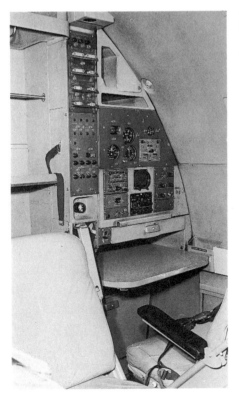

transport and the other for K tanker work — share a central computer room. In the flight deck of the tanker version there is an additional screen for the air engineer to supervise all receiving and dispensing applications. His test programmes will also incorporate possible AAR faults such as bad link ups, jammed mechanisms as well as how — when all else fails — to jettison a hose. The RAF does not take kindly to jettisoning hoses, and the air engineer trainees must remember, among other matters, to drop over open sea and not on downtown Manhatten, even though he is only on a simulator.

The six legs holding up the simulator platform and flight deck are hydrostatically controlled to provide very realistic motion cues in response to pilot inputs. The main computer, sited between the two simulators, generates audio visuals and feedbacks, and is also linked to motion system control in separate side rooms. These control areas, operated by simulator staff, incorporate micro-processor diagnostic and status monitoring. A drawbridge takes trainees and instructors on to the platform then into the flight deck. There the trainees sit at controls exactly as in an actual VC10 transport or tanker, while the instructor has a station behind them. All concerned must now concentrate extremely hard for the next three to four hours.

Assessment forms an essential yet the most difficult part of training. This is especially so when judging individuals with the high physical and mental capabilities demanded by the RAF. The system is tough at all stages and levels. One trainee said he had made 'a silly mistake' on the last day of his long course and failed the lot. So how are aircrew trainees marked? The five grades are A for exceptional, B above average, C average, D low average and E failed. In order to arrive at a worthwhile assessment, instructors are themselves instructed to look at each trainee from three viewpoints.

The first is what is called 'Airmanship'. It includes not only clear proof that the individual has 'a safe pair of hands', but also that he or she works well with the rest of the crew. Second comes 'Knowledge', full knowledge of the aircraft being operated, which means its detailed construction, systems, abilities and limitations. It is a fact that aircrews can never know enough about the planes they fly. They must keep eyes and ears open for updated equipment and unexpected phenomena. The awareness of the smallest modification is just as important as the related experience of a colleague

Loading a VC10 while wearing NBC (nuclear, biological and chemical warfare) gear.

in a storm over Sumatra. Third, the trainee must know the Task role with its alternatives and even constraints. Absorbing and becoming temporary master of each successive task is no easy matter. It calls for concentration, sometimes in crisis situations.

An Air Loadmaster in NBC gear.

'Out there', as one instructor said, 'there may be little support and few facilities'. Often crews made up of varied characters have to work with even more varied nationalities. The problems like the pressures can build up, but all have to be

A VC10 crew flying in NBC gear.

overcome. That is when the benefits of training and the qualities of leadership pay off.

No.241 OCU at Brize Norton gets through a formidable training programme every year — ten new crews for VC10s made up of transport and tankers. Annually, also, it carries out ten conversion to captain courses. In addition, the OCU is responsible for the training of all air stewards on VC10, TriStar and other aircraft, plus familiarization courses for medical officers and nurses. The planning and implementation of some 16 different types of courses is no mean task. These vary from the full conversion courses of five months duration to AAR refuelling sessions lasting three to five days. To co-ordinate everything, the Unit has a specialist adviser — a professional Education Officer — who prepares all syllabuses and arranges training aids.

The other Brize Norton aircraft, around which No.216 Squadron revolves, is the TriStar. Many outsiders ask what is the RAF doing with a civil airliner? The short answer is: a lot. The Air Force has taken the TriStar and given it some altogether different, indeed astonishing, roles. As operated by Brize, it has become another active aircraft. First of all, let us put the VC10 and TriStar side by side for comparison.

	VC10	TriStar
Aircraft Type	K2 and K3	K1 and KC1
Fuselage length	166 ft	164 ft
Wing Span	146 ft	164 ft
Tail Height	40 ft	55 ft
Power Plants	4 Conways	3 RBIIs
Total Thrust	87,200 lb	150,000 lb
Max. TO. Weight	335,000 lb	540,000 lb

A TriStar of No.216 Squadron is put through its paces.

The meaningful part, as the Americans say, is at the bottom line. Compared to the

VC10, the TriStar is a totally different asset, whereas the VC10 can carry eight pallets of freight 3,500 nautical miles, the TriStar will take 20 pallets over 5,500 miles — that is from Brize to California. There is also more to the RAF TriStars than pallets. These include passenger carrying, flight refuelling and ingenious combinations of all three as follows.

The TriStar 500 variant was the last to be built before production of this aircraft was discontinued by Lockheed. It has a slightly shorter fuselage and longer wings than earlier versions, and extra fuel tanks. The RAF acquired six TriStars from British Airways and another three from Pan Am. The six ex-BA aircraft have been converted to K MK1 and KC MK1 versions while the three ex-PA are known as C MK2s.

With the TriStar KMK1, the rear two-thirds of the passenger cabin remains unchanged and can seat up to 200 people. The forward third has special flooring fitted to hold up to 33 luggage bins. These bins are designed to be loaded through the centre passenger door. With the KCMK1, a strengthened roller conveyor floor is fitted right along the cabin and a large swing-up cargo door installed in place of the passenger one. The arrangement allows 20 pallets to be loaded. As the pallets can either carry freight or passenger seats, there is greater flexibility of aircraft usage. As for the TriStar CMK2, this is currently used for passengers only, apart from an area for stretcher cases. These three ex-Pan Am planes will carry 250 passengers and regularly do so.

The versatility of the RAF TriStars is further increased by air-to-air refuelling. The KMK1 is really a tanker with passenger-carrying capability, and the KCMK1 a fully converted tanker/freighter. Both have had refuelling probes fitted for receiving, with further fuel tanks in the forward and aft cargo holds to carry a total 137 tons of fuel. In addition, two hose drum units are installed under the rear fuselage. Thus RAF TriStar tanks can transport entire Squadron ground crews with their equipment and at the same time refuel the Squadron's fighter aircraft, all on the way to a new destination. That is Air Power!

A TriStar tanker in the Middle East.

Concorde returns to Brize Norton after a crew training exercise.

Below right Squadron Leader Eddie Cranswick who, with Bob Henderson, shared the South American flight.

Below Squadron Leader Bob Henderson. A Canadian from Vancouver, he served first in the RCAF then in the RAF. His RAF career was spent at Lyneham flying Britannias and at Brize Norton on VC10s and TriStars. He was on the TriStar which flew over the Andes and round Cape Horn as described in this chapter.

No.216 Squadron at Brize Norton has been steadily exploring and expanding these techniques. It is now quite common for the TriStars to 'tank' two or four Tornados while carrying ground crews, baggage and equipment. They regularly take combat aircraft to the Mediterranean and across the Atlantic. With the latter, each receiving plane is refuelled four times, taking on two tons of fuel at link-ups. Together they fly at 23,000 ft and the multi-aircraft crossing is achieved in five hours.

There is another bonus to the TriStars. Long distance flying is made easy by Inertial Navigation Systems (INS) coupled to a Flight Management System (FMS) computer. This ensures that, even after a flight of 5500 miles, the aircraft is within a mile of its chosen track. The system is simply programmed before take-off and, as the route is flown, the FMS automatically retunes the aircraft instruments to beacons best suited for that part of the journey. It also turns the aircraft to new courses on reaching

A view of the Andes photographed by Bob Henderson.

the various route points. Of course, the crew monitors the system all the way, but it is so reliable no navigator is needed. After take-off the human pilot switches on the autopilot and leaves it alone until nearing the destination. If the destination airfield has suitable landing aids, the TriStar is capable of a fully automatic touchdown, even in zero visibility.

Pilot and air engineers joining No.216 Squadron have to take a five months course on TriStars — two months at British Airways Training Centre near Heathrow and three at Brize. This work-packed course ends with Route Sector Training which includes transporting Service passengers to Cyprus and freight to the Falklands, assisting Army exercises in Canada and Kenya, and also tanking various aircraft. During an average year the Squadron flies some 10,000 hours. However, for operations such as the Gulf War, the flying hours increased to 1600 a month. There

An Andean range in Bob Henderson's memorable flight.

Air Chief Marshal Sir Patrick Hine enjoying flying time at RAF Brize Norton. On retiring from his 41 years of service he immediately joined the RAF Volunteer Reserve to train would-be fliers. One airman said: 'It was an honour to serve under him.'

are plans afoot to improve TriStar activities yet further, including moving all training into Brize. These aircraft are still quite young. They were among the last to be built and have plenty of life ahead of them. Thus they look like remaining with the RAF well into the next century playing many roles, as they have so far done, superbly.

There are so many fine examples of what No.216 Squadron has achieved with the Tri-Stars that it is best to concentrate on one. During the early hours of 18 June 1991 a freak rainstorm occurred over Antofagasta, a coastal town in the north of Chile. Torrents down the Andean slopes destroyed everything in their path, leaving mud up to second-storey windows. Over 100 people died and 65,000 were left homeless. To make matters worse, the next day's sun baked the mud hard and those trapped in it.

A 216 Squadron TriStar about to set off for the Falklands was immediately loaded with large tents, food and medical supplies. Whereas aircraft and crew knew their way almost blindfold to Mount Pleasant, they hastily had to rearrange another route via Brazilia, Santiago and around the Horn. The capital of Brazil was a new and magnificent sight to them, the futuristic buildings set amid a profusion of lakes. More spectacular still was their first sight of the Andes over La Paz and Lake Titicaca. They successively watched tropical jungles on the eastern slopes, canopies of rain clouds and, even though flying at 35,000 ft, they were little more than 10,000 feet above snow-capped peaks. On the final approach to Santiago, the evening sun over the Pacific turned the snowfields to an incredible pink.

The 216 TriStar touched down exactly as rescheduled after travelling well over 8000 miles. Once the load was transferred to a waiting Hercules (and a most convivial evening at the British Embassy) aircraft and crew completed the route past the Magellan Straits and on to the Falklands.

Chapter 7

MOVERS AND COMMUNICATORS

Air Transport, at its simplest definition, means using aircraft to move people and freight. The complications set in when one begins to consider the types of aircraft, the numbers of passengers, also the weights and sizes of loads to be moved. In addition, the whole effort has to be controlled by communications — all kinds of communications, forming a global network. This chapter covers some of the movers and communicators at RAF Brize Norton, and in doing so shows the extraordinary diversity of the Station. A start is made with the Operations Wing, without which nothing would move. It goes on to the RAF Movements School, which teaches the RAF and many others the principles of air movements, then gives an insight into the interesting activities of the Tactical Communications Wing.

Operations Wing

In Chapter 3 the work of RAF Brize Norton's Operations Wing was briefly introduced. The Wing not only covers the flying side, it works with many other Units, and co-ordinates all activities associated with the Station's flying task. There are three Squadrons making up this Wing — Operations, Flying Support and Air Movements. By way of a preliminary explanation it could be said that the first deals with 24 hours real time, the second is looking 24 hours ahead and beyond, whilst the third handles the actual movement of passengers and freight.

The Operations Squadron, with a staff of 40, runs the Station Ops Room on a continuous basis. Each shift is manned by a Duty Ops Controller. He and his two assistants work with movements specialists to control and co-ordinate the daily flying programme. Between them they organize and monitor every aspect of pre-flight organization and post-flight activity which is not carried out by the air crews themselves. In conjunction with many other organizations, they also monitor all movements overseas. The Operations Room, which never closes, provides a curious combination of professional expertise, good humour and — fortunately not too often — quietly managed high drama.

The second Squadron within Operations Wing, that of Flying Support, makes the longer term preparations. Most of its 16 staff have a normal working day, but its Flight Planning Section of duty personnel provides 24-hour cover. Duties of this Squadron include flight planning and flight safety, tasking and support of air transport plus the creation and maintenance of contingency plans. It is also responsible for the devising and running of Station defence exercises in conjunction with the RAF Regiment. Internally the Squadron helps to train Station personnel in flight orientated subjects, and externally it is in continuous liaison with Group and Command staffs.

The third Operations Wing Squadron, Air Movements, works from two main

Above Freight on pallet platform is pushed along a VC10 floor fitted with ball-type rollers.

locations — the Terminal Building, for passengers, and the nearby Cargo Hangar for freight. Both the terminal and hangar open on to the main concourse, variously known as the pan, apron, parking area or — to Movements people — as the 'waterfront'. As mentioned in Chapter 3, it is from this front that Operations Wing moves 15,000 passengers and 400 tons of freight a month. In wartime conditions the Wing has the added responsibility of outloading conventional weapons. The Gulf War dramatically increased the number of passengers, freight, weapons, vehicles and

Above right Typical air movements operation at Brize Norton. Loading freight into a VC10.

Another example of air movements. Backing a Land Rover into a Chinook helicopter.

all kinds of equipment leaving the 'waterfront'. At the height of Operation Granby, the personnel of Air Movements Squadron, reinforced by all who could help, was moving in three days what previously was moved in a month.

For that operation, when pantechnicons, low loaders and heavy duty trucks were converging on RAF Brize Norton at a rate of 50 or more vehicles a night, the large Cargo Hangar seemed — in the words of an Air Movements man — 'to shrink'. Two temporary hangars were erected nearby, and even then all hangars and the areas around them soon became filled with every kind of item imaginable. These items then had to be sorted, stacked and secured on pallets for loading into Service and chartered aircraft. Pallets were allocated to planes according to capacities and priorities. VC10s took eight pallets, the Tri-Stars 20 and Jumbo Jets 40.

As previously mentioned, the Operations Wing is concerned with all aspects of Station life that bear on flying activities. Recent examples were the resurfacing of runways and taxiways, the realignment of parking bays and the construction of a new system for fuelling aircraft. As one of the Operations officers wearily put it, the airfield always seemed to be full of workmen.

The Gulf conflict had a major effect on the main runway resurfacing project. For the first time ever at an RAF airfield, the runway was being resurfaced at night to allow normal — or as near normal as possible — operations during the day. However, the quantum increase in activity during the initial peak outload phase of the operation meant that contractors' work had to be stopped for the first two weeks, thereby enabling the Station to operate on a continuous basis. Thereafter the workmen were allowed back to complete the task. Thus, for the majority of the Gulf war, while the Movements people toiled through the night loading aircraft going to the Middle East, the airfield contractors workforce tackled the main runway in three stages — rip up, regrade and resurface — all two miles of it.

Operations Wing had to keep a close eye on these efforts because, from daybreak onwards heavily laden aircraft had to taxi onto and take off from the self same runway. Moreover, the work had to take many other factors into account. There were airfield lights, drainage points and a lot else besides, especially the temporary ramp angles between old and new sections of the runway. All these considerations in turn

The Land Rover, half in the helicopter, is guided and checked by movements personnel.

The Land Rover safely in a Chinook, is secured by chains and tensioners.

meant having to brief every pilot using the runway, and the briefings had to include civilian pilots who came and went during those action-packed days. At least the local population enjoyed the quiet non-flying nights.

Regarding aircraft noise, the Operations Wing and the Station's Community Relations Officer do all they can to deal with it. RAF planes have to fly, and jet engines are noisy, but flight paths and procedures can help substantially to improve the situation. Phone calls and letters are dealt with on a personal basis, often with a senior officer going to see the person concerned. At Brize Norton, as a matter of policy, Operations Wing arranges for members of neighbouring communities, as well as complainants, to fly around the local area so they can see the problem at first hand. This often results in some amusing requests such as: 'Could you fly over my house?'

Another aspect of Operations Wing work involves close liaison with two civilian manned agencies — the Meteorological Office and Customs. With regard to the first it should be mentioned that the Brize Norton Met Office is also the Group Met Office. This makes the Unit responsible for meteorological support not only at Brize but also at Benson, Boscombe Down, Farnborough, Lyneham, Manston, Northolt, Odiham, Shawbury and many other places in central and southern England. Essentially, the Met Office at Brize Norton provides a 24-hour forecasting service based on all its existing sources of weather information. The service includes face-to-face crew briefings as well as the provision of written information on overseas conditions on a 24-hour basis.

The HM Customs and Immigration services are similarly provided round the clock at Brize. Their officers based at the Station are responsible for other nearby Service and civilian airfields. Until recently, Customs control meant everyone was checked. This is now being superseded by a system like that at Heathrow, Gatwick and most other airports whereby air travellers have a choice of channels. RAF Brize Norton is approved not only for military inputs from foreign countries, but also for civilian usage. However, the latter will only be accepted with the prior approval of the Customs Officer.

Yet another aspect of Operations Wing work includes helping to update Station Ground Defence and to train teams from other Units to implement this. From time to

Backing a vehicle up the rear ramp of a Hercules aircraft. Note the nearby stool unit ready for the next air movements operation.

time, intensive two-day exercises are carried out, at which times Brize becomes a place of ultra high security. Moreover, these activities are tactically evaluated by NATO and Strike Command. The standards demanded are so high that they need months of planning and training to achieve them. At the other end of the responsibility scale, yet one which is carried out with equal thoroughness, is that of the Station's Flying Club. This is run by RAF volunteers, for the Service, but operated under Civil Aviation Authority rules and regulations. Other Ops Wing tasks include constant improvements to the Air Terminal in order to cope with the increased throughput of passengers, re-equipping the Ops Room with the latest advances in information technology, arranging the Station's Open Day for the benefit of RAF-supported charities and the reception of VIPs from all walks of life — Royalty

Use of a stool unit to help support a Hercules ramp as freight is loaded horizontally from a fork lift truck.

Above A further air movements challenge. Fitting a Harrier fuselage into a Hercules hold.

Above right Lining up the Harrier fuselage with the Hercules ramp.

and cabinet ministers at one end to business people at the other.

Whereas the passenger side of Ops Wing work tends to alternate between hyperactive arrival/departure times and relatively quiet waiting periods, life in the Cargo Hangar is continually busy. Large vans and heavy trucks keep arriving to off-load freight. Their loads have to be checked-in against documentation, then assembled according to flights and priorities. Most goods are timed to arrive some 24-36 hours before take-off so they can join others on pallets for ease of moving and aircraft loading. The Movements people do get late arrivals, and the system can handle these up to an hour before the time of departure — though no one recommends it.

The pallet system begins with an aluminium base designed to slot into the floor guidance system of its intended aircraft. The stacking of freight on to this base, usually with a fork lift truck, is both a science and an art. The stacked articles have to be relatively stable before being secured by nets, straps and tensioners to prohibit all movement in flight. To help during the stacking process, the pallet is placed on a platform which sinks into the hangar floor thus keeping the work at ground level. The weight of a stacked pallet comes to between three and four tons, and its height up to

The Harrier fuselage is carefully winched aboard.

Left A TriStar tanker at Riyadh awaits next mission. *(Courtesy of Kev Darling, BBA Photos)*

Below TriStar and Brize Norton team in desert uniform.

Brize in colour

Above A TriStar being refuelled at Brize Norton before leaving for a Falklands run.

Opposite The interior of a bulk fuel tank (before it was filled).

Left The wine glass test. An example of precision taxiing at RAF Brize Norton.

A VC10 tanker refuelling
two F16s.

Right Backing a Land
Rover into a VC10 hold.

Far right A fire fighting
exercise at Brize Norton.

Below right Aftermath.
The return of those killed
in the Gulf War.

Below Visitors to RAF
Brize Norton. A Tornado
Squadron 'drops in' for
fuel.

The Monarch's view of Brize Norton aircraft leading a Battle of Britain flypast.

7½ ft. On busy days, personnel in the Cargo Hangar can receive, stack, secure and load up to 130 pallets.

During times of national emergency Air Movements at Brize Norton receive welcome help from No.4624 (County of Oxford) Movements Squadron, an Auxiliary Air Force Unit. This pool of Movements-trained personnel is always on hand to supplement Service efforts. During the Gulf War they provided 38 additional personnel, amounting to almost half of the Movements Squadron reinforcements. More important than numbers, they represented immediate expertise in that trade. Such expertise may not be fully appreciated by the general reader, which is why the RAF Movements School at Brize Norton is covered next.

RAF Movements School

As mentioned in the Chapter 3 introduction to RAF 'movers', this School at Brize is an independent one. It is tasked directly by the Ministry of Defence, yet plays a full part in the life of the Station. The School provides movements and mobility training to personnel of the three Services, to MOD staff and forces from overseas as nominated by the Foreign and Commonwealth Office. This Establishment consists of two Flights — Training and Support, the second providing the all too important back-up to the first. School instructors are rotated through the courses, and the best of them make up what is called an Examining Cell to prepare questions and check marks.

Air Movements is a recognized Trade (18B) in the Royal Air Force, and over 20 different types of courses are run by the School to cover every aspect. The best way to appreciate the scale of the subject is to take a look at some of the courses available.

MOVEMENTS OPERATOR

This 16 week course provides the initial professional training for RAF and YTS recruits. The course size is limited to a maximum of 18 students and, by maintaining a high instructor to trainee ratio, the aim is to create interest and enthusiasm in a trade which is steadily growing in importance. Thus, classroom lessons are counterbalanced by practical lessons, and the School is located beside Brize Air Terminal and Cargo Hangar where passenger and freight movements are taking place on a daily basis.

MOVEMENTS CONTROLLER

This 6-week course forms the next stage in the training of Operators who have reached Senior Aircraftman level, and successful completion is a prerequisite for promotion to Corporal. Candidates must have received above average assessments, be recommended by their Commanding Officers and be able to pass a pre-course test. Each course takes a maximum of 12 students, and success results in qualification as a Movements Controller.

ADVANCED MOVEMENTS CONTROLLER

Movements Corporals selected for promotion to Sergeant need to graduate successfully from this three-week course. The emphasis of the course is on the managerial aspects of Air and Surface Movements. Again, only 12 students who are able to pass the pre-course test are accepted. An interesting aspect of the course is its one-week addition for those having to move explosives.

OFFICERS MOVEMENTS COURSE

This 13-week course is designed to teach Supply Officers the necessary skills and knowledge so that they are able to manage the movements of passengers, cargo and mail by air and surface means during peace and war. The successful completion of the course is a prerequisite for officers appointed to any specialist Movements post. Each course can take up to ten students of whom two may be appointed by the Foreign and Commonwealth Office.

OFFICERS MOVEMENTS REFRESHER

As its name indicates, this course provides refresher training for RAF officers who have not been employed on Movements duties for over five years, or on a required basis by an individual as a prerequisite to a future appointment. Each of these courses, which take two weeks, is tailored to suit the individual's exact needs and bring him or her completely up to date on all aspects of Movements.

Other courses available at the RAF Movements School include:

UNIT MOBILITY COURSE	1 week
ROUTE STATION TRAINING	1 week
FLIGHT DEPARTURE CONTROL	1 week
AIR MOVEMENT REINFORCEMENT	1½ weeks
DISTRICT HQ REINFORCEMENT	1½ weeks
TRISTAR DESPATCHERS COURSE	1½ weeks
ADVANCED LOAD PLANNING	3 weeks

These courses have been emphasized because they represent a necessary yet not well enough known aspect of the modern RAF. The School also runs Automatic Data Processing courses to fit in with the new Services Air Cargo System known as SACS.

The RAF Movements School at Brize Norton is next to the airfield — a dubious privilege when a VC10 or TriStar goes past. The Establishment has nine classrooms, three of which are wired up for ADP training. There is a cinema that can double as an overflow classroom and a foyer area used as a passenger reception area for the purpose of training. Nearby is the School's hangar for more practical training. It houses both a Hercules C MK1 (short) fuselage and a C MK3 (long) fuselage hold with movable ramps and doors. Beyond there is the freight half-portion of a VC10 known as the School's VC5. Unlike the Hercules with its inclined ramp, the VC10 and TriStar freight doors are some 20ft up in the air, thus presenting their own sets of loading problems.

To help trainees learn about and overcome all conceivable problems, there are typical loads of every shape, size and weight ranged round the insides of the School hangar, and more outside. These dummy loads include several hundred suitcases and ammunition boxes, various vehicles, jet engines on their stands, missile packs, oil drums, power-generating sets and, of course, pallets. The last have to be stacked, netted and secured, then loaded into the aircraft holds. These examples give a good idea on the complexities and infinite variety of air movements. Trainees at the School have to carry out practice runs of all types of freight handling and loading — with their efforts timed to the second.

Video monitoring plays an important part in the work of the School so that trainees can, after their exertions, see what they did right and wrong. These monitors are fitted both in the School foyer cum passenger reception area and in the hangar. In the case of passenger handling, the student behind the reception desk has to keep his cool and maintain eye contact while dealing with the intricacies of a computerized reservation system, and often the peculiarities of certain passengers. Instructors acting as VIPs, pregnant women, medical cases and even the slightly inebriated try to show the trainees what can but should never be allowed to go wrong.

The Officers' Movements Course culminates in a detachment, often abroad, where students actually unload, reload and turn round aircraft. This adds another training factor — the real risk of delay if he or she makes mistakes. Regarding the 'she' part of the last sentence, it should be noted here that more and more women are entering what was once a male preserve. At one time there was a great deal of physical work involved, but with mechanized handling and computerized control the ladies are proving their worth, especially with their eye to detail and 'good housekeeping'.

An essential part of the RAF Movements School takes place in 'the back room'. The School support team has to work a year ahead, matching the programme of courses with the numbers of instructors, and the availability of classrooms, computers, simulators and other School equipment. Instruction packs of data, diagrams, slides, vugraphs and video films all have to be prepared and kept up-to-date. This is a continual process reflecting the ever changing nature of the Movements business. Such support frees instructors from the burden of updating lessons, so they can concentrate on their primary function of teaching.

During Operation Granby, the RAF Movements School's six officers and 24 NCOs, with a wealth of experience between them, cancelled all but a few of the more important courses and turned their hands to the formidable tasks facing the Station. One of the more difficult tasks they took over was that of looking after possible heavy casualties. To this end they formed teams for the reception and smooth turnround of aeromedical evacuation aircraft at 20 airports all over the country. Moreover, they established handling procedures with the National Health Service, the police and other civilian bodies. Fortunately most of these arrangements were not needed.

Turning now to the lighter side of Air Movements life, the School, like other Units at Brize, takes a pride in supporting a charity. In the case of RAFMS the charity is the National Children's Home, and one method recently used to raise funds is so ingenious it deserves mention here. In fact, if there was a Nobel Prize for inspired thinking, the School should receive it. The scheme is related here because it will also tell readers a great deal more about the spirit of the Station.

The episode started with a gift of four teddy bears. To make them more interesting they were given the names of Amy Millicent, Alison Matilda, Augustus Marvin and Alistair Marmaduke, with the surname of Way. Each teddy bear then acquired an as yet empty portfolio and a mock passport. It was decided the bears should visit modern historical sites where they would be photographed. Pictures and details of their

Below left The fund-raising bears await their helicopter flight.

Below Squadron Leader Henry *(left)* and School officers with teddy bears that made air movements and fund-raising history.

Above The bears arrive in Washington DC.

travels were to be entered into the portfolios so that, when the four bears were auctioned for charity, they would fetch a better contribution.

The historical sites selected were Berlin, because of its Wall; the Falklands, because of that war; Hong Kong on account of imminent return to China; and Washington DC, capital of the Free World in the East/West disarmament talks. So the bears began with the visit to Berlin where each wisely spent pocket money in purchasing a boxed piece of the Wall. Next they flew in a 216 Squadron TriStar to the Falklands and were featured in the world's most southerly newspaper — *The Southern Star*. On their way back they stopped off at Ascension Island for a 3000 ft climb to the top of Green Mountain, for which feat each teddy earned a certificate of achievement. On their visit to Hong Kong the immigration officer wrote his greetings on the bears' passports — in Chinese. As for the visit to Washington, the bears insisted on being photographed outside the Capitol building because the White House was then covered in scaffolding and the President was away at the time.

One might suspect that all these excursions were going to the bears' heads. Let us say they were well pleased and asked for more prior to the auction. So they went to Calgary in Canada where they were introduced to some of their grizzly cousins, then they continued to Alaska, Australia, India, the Middle East and eventually home again. Lest official eyebrows might be raised at these peregrinations, it should be emphasized that the bears only accompanied those travelling on accredited business. Nevertheless they always managed to be treated as VIPs, perhaps because of such notable feats as flying with the Red Arrows and free-fall parachuting with the Falcons.

Although too young to know much about the Battle of Britain, the bears were keen to take part in the anniversary celebration. Parading and marching did not appeal to them. Only a flight would do, and for such experienced flyers the best was demanded. Consequently they flew over Buckingham Palace in the Battle of Britain Memorial Flight Lancaster — *The City of Lincoln*. While in London they went to the House of Lords and had tea with Lord Murray of Epping before visiting the Bahamas with the Princess Royal. For a final fling the bears went round a Formula One Motor Racing Circuit to add yet another certificate to their portfolios.

Above right Each bear did a parachute jump with an RAF Falcon.

Eventually the time came to auction the bears — with their well-stamped passports, bulging portfolios and over 100,000 miles flown in every case. Each bidder was asked to make his or her bid, preferably as a cheque payable to the National

Children's Home. With this kind of auction, all bids go into a kitty and the highest secures a bear. Thus the bids went to the charity while the winning ones did not have to be excessive. As for the bears, they have since been content to rest on their laurels while fans continue to admire them and their impressive documentation.

To end this account of Brize Movers on a serious note, every air transport flight requires detailed planning and actioning, not the least of which are the movements of passengers and freight. Many forms of communication are also needed, and the contribution made by the Tactical Communication Wing has been selected because it is not sufficiently known outside Service circles.

Below left A TCW technician in battle gear checks a generator powering communications equipment.

Tactical Communications Wing

The Tactical Communications Wing at Brize Norton is made up of RAF and Army personnel working closely and cheerfully together. Their relative strengths are 250 RAF and 120 Army. The RAF contingent is divided into two Squadrons that are, in turn, made up of flights. These Squadrons are designated Base Support and Field Communications.

Starting with the RAF's Base Support Squadron, this has four flights as follows:

1. BASE ENGINEERS. This flight looks after all ground communications equipment, such as airfield radar, and has its own transportable Units.

2. ENGINEERING SUPPORT. This flight has a repair facility to maintain equipment in Service usage. It also has a Development Section to deal with the introduction of new equipment into service.

3. STANDARDS AND TRAINING. All new arrivals to the Wing go through a month's tuition in field procedures, which means how to operate anywhere in the world under all types of conditions.

Below The hard graft of Tactical Communications Wing. Building a base at Dahran during the Gulf War.

4. OPERATIONS. This flight co-ordinates the work of the Base Support Squadron and much of the Tactical Communications Wing. Tasks emanating from the

TCW technician armed and using signalling equipment.

Ministry of Defence and Strike Command, via No.1 Group, are first passed to Ops Flight for assessment of what is required by way of manpower and equipment.

The other TCW Squadron, Field Communications, is divided into two flights. The first, MOBILE COMMUNICATIONS, consists of three-man detachments operating over short distances, by which they mean Northern Europe. These detachments are ready, rationed and equipped to move out and set up VHF and HF field communications posts whenever needed. The second, STRATEGIC

TCW motor cyclists.

A youngster learning about TCW activities.

COMMUNICATIONS, works worldwide via HF satellite communications. It is ever ready for 'the real thing'— such as the Gulf War.

In the past two decades, Tactical Communications Wing has deployed (alphabetically) to — Ascension, Australia, Barbados, Belgium, Belize, Canada, Cyprus, Denmark, Falklands, France, Germany, Hong Kong, Indonesia, Iraq, Italy, Kenya, Lebanon, Nepal, New Zealand, Norway, Portugal, Saudi Arabia, Shetlands, Turkey, USA, and other places it is not mentioning. So it is a case of joining TCW and seeing most of the world.

Apart from keeping personnel and equipment in constant readiness, TCW members take part in regular and rigorous exercises to prove their efficiency. For example, the airfield radar equipment is suddenly sent to a remote location like the Outer Hebrides. The detachment consists of six to seven vehicles, with radar and generators, accompanied by ten men with tents and rations. They have time targets to meet while travelling and setting up the equipment which is then tested by RAF aircraft over a period of up to three weeks.

If that sounds straightforward, another Tactical Communications Wing exercise involves survival in Arctic conditions away from airfields or even human habitation. Again six to seven vehicles, each manned by three people, go to northern Norway in January/February when the weather is at its most inhospitable. The vehicles are Land Rovers in which are fitted hand-operated signals equipment. Personnel then have to live in and around the Land Rovers, maintaining a 24-hour state of alertness by having one man on radio watch, one on guard and one sleeping.

When the Gulf situation began to develop, the first Units of Tactical Communication Wing were out there and in place within days. Subsequently they were deployed at every airfield and in forward areas during Operations Granby, Desert Storm and Haven. In such circumstances, every Service aircraft flying is backed by TCW support, and for major operations over 90% of the Wing will be where the action is.

Chapter 8

ATTACKERS AND DEFENDERS

The title of this chapter encapsulates the activities of two Units at RAF Brize Norton — No.1 Parachute Training School and No.19 Squadron RAF Regiment. Currently, the Units are not engaged in attacking or defending, also they do a great deal more as will be described. Ultimately, however, airborne forces are trained to attack, and the RAF Regiment to defend, airfields. Once this simplification is understood, then the full range of activities carried out by both Units can be better appreciated.

No.1 Parachute Training School

In Chapter 2 it was mentioned that the school came to Brize Norton in 1976, and in Chapter 3 a brief introduction was made. The time has come to make more impact because No.1 Parachute Training School is one of the most impressive and inspiring Units at RAF Brize Norton. Where to begin? Well, for impact, a newcomer only has to walk into the School's training hangar. Outside it looks quiet and relaxed like the rest of the Station, until the planes go past. Inside, it is what can only be described as solid noise echoing and re-echoing with the clear-cut commands of the instructors,

Training to become a parachutist begins at floor level. A trainee learning how to fall and roll.

112

Trainee paratroopers practising exit drill.

the shouted responses from troops of men, the clatter of training apparatus and the thuds of pupils' bodies on the hangar floor.

It all seems incomprehensible until the whole process of parachuting is analysed. Anyone can fall down and be hurt, or slip off a mere chair and break a limb, yet the inherent dangers do not multiply at 30 ft, 800 ft, 2000 ft or 12,000 ft. As an instructor put it: 'It's still the landing that hurts.' Nevertheless, man has an equally inherent fear of falling, which brings one to the crest and motto of No.1 Parachute Training School — 'Knowledge Dispels Fear'.

What is going on in that noisy hangar is the instillation of knowledge which the parachute jumping instructors (PJIs) have themselves acquired. Trainees start

Below left Landing training — an essential drill.

Below Landing training continues under the watchful eye of an RAF instructor.

Above Exiting from a fan descent trainer is the next 40 ft step to becoming a paratrooper.

learning to fall with their feet firmly on the floor — or rather on a mat. They keep their legs together as they collapse and roll, over and over again, until they do it instinctively. Only then do they go up a step, put on a parachute, and get the feel of the harness. Their first real taste of jumping comes from what is called the Fan Trainer. This is a Hercules fuselage mock-up 40 ft above the hangar floor. The trainee's harness is attached to a cable. When he drops from the doorway his descent is slowed by the paddle wheels of a fan to which the other end of the cable is attached. Thus his rate of descent is controlled to that of an actual parachute landing. Once more the trainees have to do this over and over again until they get it right.

Trainees then move outdoors to a 40 ft-high structure near to the main gate. This outdoor exit trainer, to use its official name, allows the still-tethered trainee to drop a fair distance until his harness pulls him up with a jerk. It is also commonly called the 'knacker-cracker' for obvious reasons.

Following indoor and outdoor training, which has taken students up to about 40 ft, they now go to the balloon at nearby RAF Weston-on-the-Green for jumps of 800 ft. Newcomers say this is the hardest part, but training should have made it a reflex action to jump on order. The parachute is opened automatically via a static line, after which the trainee steers it away from the balloon cable as he has been taught. All too soon he is coming into land which he does in a rolling movement as learned in the hangar.

After the balloon descent, trainees spend another three days on further ground training before commencing the first of seven jumps from a Hercules aircraft. They enter the aircraft hold sixty at a time and sit down in rows. In due course the side doors are opened, equipment is hooked up and checked with each man shouting until the one at the front of the 'stick' calls 'Port . . .' or 'Starboard Stick OK!' A parachute jumping instructor, acting as a despatcher (or chucker-out) also checks every

Above right Jumping from a balloon at 800 ft is the most difficult part of parachute training.

individual and item of equipment. The stick shuffles forward, because each man is burdened with heavy equipment making individual weights up to 14 stone. After the troops have left the aircraft, at intervals of one second, the despatcher and his helpers have to pull in all the static lines and empty parachute covers. As should now be appreciated, becoming a paratrooper is a rough, tough, physical existence.

Which explains why such insistence is laid on physical fitness, and why — from 1941 — only RAF physical training instructors were trained to become parachute jumping instructors. The progress of parachuting, especially as practised by the School, is also one of technical refinements. In parallel with thousands of Regular and Territorial Army soldiers being trained annually, School personnel are involved in the development of parachuting techniques, testing new equipment and taking part in many associated activities.

But to continue with the basic training of military static line parachutists. They have six more practice jumps from aircraft, and have to undergo more training before receiving their coveted wings. Up to the Wings Parade a recruit can drop out. After that the paratrooper must jump when ordered. The ceremony, following four weeks of physical strain and mental stress, is a moving one because the men have entered an airborne brotherhood. They are now members of a special fraternity recognized worldwide. And yet, in parachuting terms, this is only a beginning.

There still are the highly complex techniques of conveying heavy equipment like inflatable craft, guns, ammunition and vehicles from aircraft to ground or sea level; of free falling; of high altitude, low opening; of sports parachuting; of helicopter operations; winter landings; of intricate formation descents. To put inflatable boats as well as arms, munitions, supplies and even diving gear, safely down in the sea at night below the level of enemy radar involves planning and mathematics rather than a macho image.

How is it all done? A brief look back at how the Parachute School evolved will prove part of the answer. Parachuting is not new. Men have dreamed of it over the centuries and made various attempts, most of which proved disastrous. Yet, surprisingly, the first successful parachute descent in England took place as far back as 1802. It was done by a Frenchman, Andre Jacques Garnerin, using a balloon and a semi-rigid parachute. He parachuted from no less than 8,000 ft and it took him 10 minutes 20 seconds. The art was resurrected during World War I when observers, lifted aloft by balloons, parachuted to safety when attacked. Between the wars, while

Far left After a static line opens the parachute the trainee steers it away from the balloon cable as he has been taught.

Left Trainees completing their jump from the balloon.

many countries — notably France, Germany and Russia — took military parachuting seriously, Britain dabbled with a few parachutists being pulled off the wings of various Vickers and Handley Page aircraft. It was more an 'air circus stunt' and, interestingly, many such stuntmen became parachute instructors.

A notable date in the history of British parachuting was 6 June 1940 when Winston Churchill wrote the following directive to his Chiefs of Staffs:

'We ought to have a Corps of at least 5,000 parachute troops. Pray let me have a note from the War Office on this subject.'

That was less than a month after the fall of France when Churchill, if not the War Office, had seen what the enemy achieved with their parachutists. As a result of his directive it was decided to form a School for military parachutists — originally called a Central Landing Establishment — at Ringway Airport. The Royal Air Force was tasked to set up and run the School which it has done ever since.

RAF Henlow, until then the home of parachuting, agreed to lend Ringway two pilots, ten airmen and a modified Whitley bomber. The tail turret was removed first for pull-off descents, which were discontinued after a few weeks. The lower fuselage gun turret, known as the dustbin, was then taken out to make an aperture through which a parachutist could drop. After that a dropping zone was chosen at a private estate some five miles from Ringway. Nevertheless, as someone said at the time: 'Britain had no suitable aircraft, no proper parachute, no training system and no previous knowledge.'

In April 1941, Winston Churchill visited Ringway and was impressed — particularly as the wind kept exceeding 25 mph, which in those days was the top limit for parachuting. Forty troops were dropped, and a hundred more, hiding in the grass beside the airfield, helped the parachutists to collapse their 28 ft diameter chutes. Then 140 troops joined in a mock attack towards the VIPs. It was all a little haphazard and often more than a little dangerous, but techniques improved. One key decision made then applies to this day. The War Office gave approval for the RAF to carry out such training, and instructors were henceforth drawn from the Air Force's Physical Training Branch. Meanwhile, WAAF parachute packers worked long hours maintaining the flow of chutes to the school and paratroop forces.

Over a hectic period of exactly four years, from 6 June 1940 to D-Day 6 June 1944, the Ringway School and Tatton Park Drop Zone trained parachutists day and night, including weekends. A thousand men at a time took the course and everyone knew they would be needed for the invasion of Nazi-occupied Europe. To paratroopers this meant drops on Normandy, at Arnhem and across the Rhine, with everything each operation implied. For the school's part, it trained 60,000 British and Allied parachutists and over 400,000 descents were made.

During and after the war in Europe, paratroop operations were also required in the Middle East and Far East. The latter involvement bought school instructors in contact with the Gurkhas and gave rise to a now famous story. These gallant soldiers were glad that the training aircraft would be flying at 200 ft rather than 600 ft — not realizing they were to have parachutes.

However, Far Eastern operations were serious ones with drops into high mountains and into deep jungles. Following their descents at the centres of terrorist held areas, the Special Forces had to fight themselves out. Only parachutists could and did do it.

Meanwhile, the Parachute Training School was on the move from Ringway to Upper Heyford (1945-1950), then to Abingdon (1950-1975). Training techniques also progressed to double-door jumping from Hastings aircraft. In 1954, six RAF instructors were chosen for the British Free Fall Team in the World Parachute Championships. In 1955 reserve parachutes strapped to the chest came into regular use. Not everyone liked the reserve because parachutists could no longer see their feet when coming in for stand-up landings. By 1965, the Falcons, made up of RAF

Far left RAF Falcons display a perfect canopy stack.

Left Paratroopers watch the Falcons demonstrate finer points.

parachute instructors, were a well-established team. In due course the use of round chutes was augmented by the 'squares' and the latter went through full Service trials — at No.1 Parachute Training School. The school came to RAF Brize Norton in April 1976 and has continued the military parachute training of all Army, Royal Marines and RAF regiments.

Such then is the background of No.1 Parachute Training School. What of the place itself? How is it organized and run? The school is made up of two training Squadrons and one support Squadron. Training Squadrons are named Static Line and Free Fall, which describes their ultimate functions. However, a great deal goes on before trainees put on parachutes and jump out of aircraft. No.1 PTS runs a solid training programme that covers the whole year ahead and consists of 16 different courses.

Starting with the regular basic course already described, this trains newcomers for the Army Parachute Regiment, Royal Marines, Royal Air Force — in fact, all those

Below RAF Falcons show their skills. They will land on the crosses in the area to the left of the tower.

Prince Charles, who trained at No.1 Parachute School, Brize Norton, about to make his first balloon descent.

who have not previously parachuted. There are 12 such courses a year, the course lasts for four weeks and up to 60 people attend each. After ground and balloon training there are seven jumps from aircraft including one at night. The School also runs a Territorial Army (TA) Course of two weeks, 15 times a year. This course is taken by personnel of the Airborne Territorial Army and Royal Marines reserve Units honing their skills. It also incorporates seven descents from aircraft, though not one at night. Many of the refresher courses involve the School's instructors either being permanently detached or going to other Units. Owing to TA involvement, much of this work takes place at weekends.

Other PTS courses include training Royal Marines how best to parachute together with equipment such as inflatable boats and signalling gear. There are courses for training instructors (19 weeks plus a six months probationary period), courses for parachuting from helicopter and courses for aircrew having to parachute into the sea. The Military Free Fall course takes six weeks and involves, among other refinements, parachuting with oxygen from 25,000 ft. These MFF courses are taken by elements of Special Forces including the SAS, SBS and two Pathfinders of the 5th Army Brigade who in wartime conditions would have to go in first and set up dropping zones for the rest of the paratroops.

It is difficult and perhaps unfair to single out certain aspects of the School's many activities, yet one such subject is the work done at Weston-on-the-Green. Apart from this airfield being a military zone for static line, balloon drops and free fall descents, it

Prince Andrew went
through the same course.

is also used by the RAF Sports Parachute Association and the Joint Services Adventurous Training Courses. At weekends, sport parachuting is also open to civilians. Most people's introduction to the sport is either via a tandem descent (strapped to an instructor) or an accelerated freefall course (with two instructors who maintain a hold throughout the free fall). On further descents the student, still accompanied by instructors, opens the chute. The word 'accelerated' for this course refers to the speed of learning.

So far little has been said about free fall. The majority of military parachute descents involve jumping from aircraft at 600-1000 ft using a round parachute which is opened automatically, by a line attached inside the aircraft. Only experienced parachutists progress to the more advanced techniques taught by the School's Free Fall Squadron. There are several free fall courses a year, and much of this highly specialized training takes place abroad — notably in California, south-west France and Portugal — where the weather is kinder than in Britain.

A military application of free fall is High Altitude Low Opening (HALO) developed to deliver teams behind enemy lines. These parachutists leave their aircraft from as high as 25,000 ft where it takes them ten seconds to reach their terminal velocity of 120 mph. After that they free fall for nearly two minutes until opening their chutes at 3,000 ft. A further three to four minutes descent follows before they arrive. To jump from 25,000 ft requires thermal clothing and oxygen — the whole outfit, with other equipment, supplies, arms and ammunition making movement difficult. During daylight at 25,000 ft parachutists can see a slight curvature of the earth. At night, they are alone with the moon and stars, but they can see each other as each team member uses special lights which give a green phosphorescent glow.

At No.1 Parachute Training School a further means of training is to become a member of the RAF Falcons. This is a high profile, prestigious job symbolizing the Royal Air Force's mastery of the air. The Falcons team consists of 15 men — three officers including the team leader, one Flight Sergeant as team coach, one Sergeant looking after safety equipment and ten Sergeants who help put on astonishing free fall displays. Each year the Falcons perform up to 100 public displays which are backed by 200 or more training descents. They use Hercules, Andovers and rotary wing aircraft whenever possible as jump platforms. In turn the RAF maintains three categorized aircrews, all of whom have been trained to work with and drop the Falcons.

Although the Falcons have put on displays around the world, the majority of these take place in the United Kingdom where the primary objective is to encourage RAF recruitment. Each drop is different and meticulously planned. The Falcons' team leader briefs the aircrew as to what is required. This briefing uses aerial photographs of the dropping zone and high specification maps. Weather conditions, radio frequencies and despatch procedures all come into the detailed briefings. Even before the Falcons' aerial team sets out, its ground team will be in position to establish contact with the aircraft and to make many necessary preparations.

The Falcons' ground team releases and tracks three helium-filled balloons using a theodolite to plot wind speeds and directions with the utmost accuracy. This data is relayed to the aircraft captain and Falcon team leader so that the run in and release point can be plotted. A ground flare indicates the drop zone to the aircraft approaching at heights of between 2,200 and 12,000 ft, and smoke from the flare confirms the direction of surface wind. Next to be seen are two crosses on the ground, made of red and yellow fabric, which mark the impact point.

At the exact moment reached by calculation and experience, the Falcons actuate their smoke canisters and jump. Jumping from the prearranged height they free fall before deploying their chutes (called canopies) and forming up into a canopy stack. It is usual team practice for the top half of the stack to spiral to the left while the bottom half spirals to the right. The approach invariably captures the attention of every crowd. The Falcons are also in radio communication, so that they can co-ordinate their moves, and they land at five second intervals, alternately on the red and yellow crosses. There they release their canopies, remove smoke canisters, pull on RAF berets and line up for a salute as the aircraft flies overhead, to applause from the crowd.

Every descent by the Falcons is recorded on video from start to finish so that team members can evaluate their own performances at a debriefing. They are the best of the best, yet always learning. What can eventually be accomplished was demonstrated when an international team of 30 parachutists formed five linked rings of different colours and descended into the Los Angeles Olympic Stadium. Naturally they included and were coached by an instructor from No.1 Parachute Training School at RAF Brize Norton.

Before leaving this inspiring Establishment, mention must be made of the School Parachute Museum. The museum is unique in that it covers over 50 years of No.1 PTS history, together with many other aspects of parachuting. Collections and donations have brought together a wealth of material ranging from photographs and historic equipment to log books, diaries, newspaper cuttings and items from many other allied and one-time enemy sources. Just to stand in the museum is to be rewarded with a feeling of endeavour and bravery. Since its inception No.1 Parachute Training School has trained parachutists from 43 different nations, as well as UK forces. During an average year 2,500 trainees pass through the school. Together, with

Members of No.19 Squadron RAF Regiment honing their skills at battle camp.

their instructors, they make over 40,000 jumps. It is an impressive figure for an impressive place.

No.19 Squadron RAF Regiment

In Chapter 3 reference was made to this Squadron, the largest of all the RAF Regiment's Rapier Units, which is lodged at Brize Norton. The primary role of the Regiment is to defend RAF airfields, and it has in recent years provided such services

Battle camp exercise in NBC (nuclear, biological and chemical warfare) gear.

Rapier fire Unit — one of the silent guards at Britain's airfields.

to UK Stations being used by the US Air Force. No.19 Squadron specifically provides short-range air defence at RAF Upper Heyford and RAF Fairford where US aircraft are currently operating. Thus the close understanding which has always existed between the RAF and the USAF is extended to the defence of those airbases against enemy air attack — a vital factor in the total operational concept. It is also another example of how Units based at Brize Norton fit into a much larger picture.

No.19 Squadron RAF Regiment is situated on the far side of Brize airfield. As one drives towards it, a large headquarters building together with a much large hangar comes into view. The quiet orderliness of the surrounds — neatly parked cars, Land Rovers and trucks — belies the brisk activities taking place in both buildings. For No.19, which has 188 men including 11 officers and 25 senior NCOs, is a very active Unit, as will be described. It is also a very technical Unit. Like many modern forces, the wearing of camouflage clothing conceals the presence of highly trained mechanical and electronic engineers.

No.19 Squadron itself has 42 such technicians, nearly a quarter of its total strength. Moreover, all personnel are trained in a range of defence skills starting with the Rapier system then extending to arms, armaments and the latest counter-measures against nuclear, biological and chemical (NBC) attacks. They are also well versed in anti-terrorist techniques and kept alert by tests and exercises. Recruitment at RAF Swinderby is very selective, and basic training at the Regiment's RAF Catterick depot is tough. Newcomers then go on to training with the Rapier system and, to prove themselves proficient with all aspects, operatives have to keep swopping tasks so that everybody is capable. Only then do they move to a Squadron like No.19 at Brize Norton.

The Squadron is equipped with 12 Rapier fire Units, each with an eight-man crew. The crew consists of a well-experienced Sergeant as its detachment commander, two equally well-experienced Corporals as tactical controllers, and five operators. No.19 is organized into five flights. Its Headquarters flight provides five command and control posts, then there are three Rapier flights, each of four fire Units. Finally there is the Engineering flight. The latter is needed to look after the technically sophisticated equipment and the Squadron's fleet of over 140 vehicles which gives it mobility and flexibility.

The focus of operations, as applied to No.19 Squadron, involves defence of the USAF at RAF Upper Heyford and Fairford as two separate entities. As previously stated, the Squadron's fire Units are tasked with providing short-range air defence (SHORAD). If an airfield is attacked by air they will respond by firing their Rapier missiles. RAF Upper Heyford is the home of the USAF's 20th Tactical Fighter wing with four F-111 Squadrons, whereas RAF Fairford hosts temporary deployments of Strategic Air Command B-52 bombers. No.19 retains its full defence role, despite the recent relaxation in East/West relations, putting both airfields and aircraft on a standby basis.

Instant response is the name of the defence game, and 19 Squadron has again and again proved its effectiveness and flexibility during NATO tactical evaluations (TACEVALS). In addition, the Squadron conducts its own tests and exercises every few months and the most thorough examination every 18 months during TACEVAL. The Squadron also keeps itself proficient in infantry skills by deployment to battle camps where individual and collective skills are practised.

The Rapier guided weapon system was originally designed to provide air defence cover for the Army in the field, but is also used by the RAF, for protecting airfields. It can deal with fast low flying aircraft and helicopters, either directly approaching or crossing, at heights up to 10,000 ft. The system Units are air-portable by both fixed and rotary wing aircraft, as well as highly mobile on the ground, being compact and lightweight. No outside fire control inputs are required, so Rapiers can be deployed in the number of fire Units and configuration the situation demands.

RAF Regiment personnel were closely involved in the initial user trials of the Rapier system which is manufactured by British Aerospace. The first RAF Regiment Rapier Squadron was formed in 1972 and the first four Squadrons were deployed to defend RAF Germany airfields assigned to NATO. The system was subsequently developed so that it could track both the target and missile, which resulted in the addition of night and poor-weather capabilities. By 1981, all RAF Regiment Rapier Squadrons were equipped with the combined versions, and an advanced system is on its way to take airfield defence into the next century.

With the present improved system the target is identified by the radar which then tracks it. Target position data is then fed to a computer in the launcher Unit. The

Firing Rapier missiles at a range in the Outer Hebrides.

Above RAF Regiment training with live ammunition.

Above right A member of 19 Squadron RAF Regiment on guard duty.

computer evaluates the stream of information received and informs the operator when to fire the missile. Once launched, both the missile and target are tracked, the former being guided at the latter by computer commands. Accuracy of the Rapier system is in excess of 70%.

Returning to the subject of training, 19 Squadron RAF Regiment conducts a rigorous programme to retain fitness for its primary role. The annual missile practice camp is usually at the Royal Artillery range in the Outer Hebrides. There the teams set up and fire the missile under operation conditions. These engagements are carried out in both optical and radar modes and some 75 missiles are fired at two different types of targets — towed and remote controlled.

The Squadron also participates in exercises held in other NATO countries where it meets and competes against various forces and airfield defence systems. The last such visit was to the Royal Danish Air Force where the Squadron was deployed for two weeks. Nato aircraft such as the Draken, F16, Harrier, Jaguar, Tornado, A10, F4 and Alpha Jet 'attacked' the defenders. Apart from 19 Squadron with its Rapiers, the defenders included the Danes and Norwegians with their Hawk systems, the Germans with Roland and the Dutch with Patriot — a truly European defence exercise.

Chapter 9

AEROMEDICAL SERVICES

Included among the Medical and Dental Units at RAF Brize Norton is a modest building with a signboard bearing the enigmatic name of Aeromedical Evacuation Training Centre. It is a title that one might notice in passing then forget the next minute. However, those who have been on the receiving end of the RAF's aeromedical services are full of praise. This Centre and what it does represents yet another facet of Station life.

The transport of casualties by air goes back further than most people will guess and — praise where honour is due — the French started it in 1870. During the Siege of Paris a total of 160 patients were successfully evacuated by balloon. The first recorded case of a casualty transported via aircraft was in 1915 when a French captain successfully flew a wounded airman to safety. During 1918 in Morocco the French used air ambulances.

Around the same time the RAF in Egypt began what was to become an on-going development programme of aeromedical transportation. A medical officer designed a modification of the DH6 whereby a fairing behind the passenger seat was cut away to allow space for a general service stretcher. In 1919, during the Somaliland campaign, the Air Force transported three patients on stretchers fixed inside the tail end of a DH9 fuselage.

At this point in aeromedical progress Brize's 216 Squadron enters the story. During the early 1920s one of the Squadron's Vikers Vimy aircraft was allocated for the purpose of evacuating emergency medical cases from isolated areas. This particular plan displayed the Red Cross. However, not long afterwards, the Air Force decided to remove the sign because it restricted the use of the aircraft for other roles. In the main the RAF has modified aircraft for fitting stretchers as and when required and used the Red Cross only on specific agreed occasions.

During 1923 Vickers Vernons and Victories of Nos.45 and 70 Squadrons carried some 389 patients out of Kurdistan to an RAF Hospital near Baghdad. Through 1924 the Air Force moved 88 patients by air in Iraq, and also during 1924 the first air ambulance service in the United Kingdom was started at RAF Halton. Between 1925 and 1938, a total of 2,112 patients were transported by the RAF. The majority of these went in troop-carrying aircraft so constructed as to be converted into flying ambulances at short notice.

By the end of World War II, the RAF had carried approximately 400,000 patients in all theatres and, in doing so, had undertaken 30,000 such flights without mishap. Throughout the latter stages of European operations, 90% of casualties were transported by air. Since 1945 the RAF has carried out aeromedical flights almost on a continuous basis around the world. The Falklands campaign, for example, necessitated the air transportation of about 1,000 casualties over the long stretches of

An aeromedical team
dealing with a casualty
situation.

the South Atlantic.

The present-day RAF aeromedical task, to which Brize Norton makes a significant contribution, is a highly adaptable one. While all the Service stops are pulled out for emergencies, use is made of civil airline and charter services. Their competitive costs are far cheaper than sending military aircraft. In the case of British military concentrations — Germany, Cyprus and the Falklands — RAF planes, many of them from Brize Norton — carry out these aeromedical duties.

Medical personnel and equipment are on constant call within the United Kingdom. When a medical officer overseas requires an aircraft to move a patient, he advises the RAF's aeromedical Unit at High Wycombe. He states the urgency of the case together with other information such as emplaning and deplaning airfields, reception hospital and nursing staff required. Urgent cases can be moved almost immediately, whereas years ago patients, from say the Far East, faced a sea voyage of about six weeks. Today, thanks to the RAF Aeromedical Services they can be flown home under expert medical care and admitted to a hospital or rehabilitation Unit in 24 hours.

These services do not run purely on compassion and by chance. Like everything else in the RAF, there is much organization and training. A chain of command outlines specific responsibilities in regard to aeromedical policy, its structure and control. To those who have to assess and decide on these matters, several options immediately become apparent. A key question is 'what sort of air transport should be used for the patient(s)?' The choice includes scheduled aeromedical flights, passenger-cum-freighter flights, other flights already tasked, special flights, helicopters, MOD chartered flights and civilian flights.

Then there is the make-up of the aeromedical team. Such a team may comprise a combination of Flight Nursing Officers, Flight Nursing Attendants, Registered Mental Nurses, Medical Officers and Medical/Theatre Technicians. The team leader is automatically the most senior person by rank, and he or she is responsible to the aircraft captain. Following the formation of the aeromedical team, each member has clear-cut duties. These considerable responsibilities include the maintenance of patients' notes, X-rays, personal documentation and special equipment needed; liaison with the hospitals, in-flight nursing and continuation of treatment to prevent deterioration of the patient's condition. Other duties consist of checking and stowing aeromedical equipment. Lengthy lists are made to cover every eventuality.

Before any aeromedical movement takes place there has to be a clinical assessment. While it has been found from long experience that there are few patients who cannot be transported by air in pressurized aircraft using specially developed equipment, the decision to initiate this procedure is one of assessment. In parallel with assessing the clinical criteria, many aviation factors have also to be taken into consideration — suitable facilities both in flight and at staging posts, together with the proposed altitude and duration of the flight itself.

Often special arrangements have to be made such as for patients in the infectious stage of serious communicable diseases. When carrying infectious cases, precautions

Ambulance men bring a stretcher on to an aircraft.

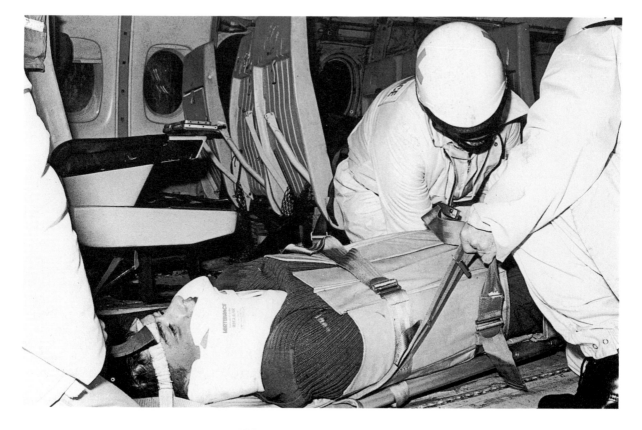

Preparing an infectious
patient for flight.

have to be taken for protecting other patients, passengers and crew. The RAF aeromedical teams are trained to handle the widest possible range of patients suffering from respiratory problems, cardiac failures, wounds, broken limbs, haemorrhages, anaemia and detached retinas — to quote but a few. There are also medical considerations when air transporting pregnant women after the 32nd week of pregnancy, infants sometimes under one month old and needing respirators, handicapped people and mentally disturbed patients. Psychiatric patients may have to be kept under sedation before and during the flight, also restraint equipment will be

Lifting and moving an
infectious patient into a
VC10.

Lifting a Red Cross Unit for access to an aircraft door.

available on the aircraft. Every case, as the aeromedical people keep emphasizing, is different.

In order to assess priority cases, each patient considered for aeromedical transportation is evaluated by the medical officer responsible and the details entered in his clinical documents. There are four priorities and several classifications. Priority one is life-saving and calls for 24 hour return to the United Kingdom. Priority two covers speedy transfer cases and the return time can be up to 48 hours. Priority three is for those patients who, while receiving adequate local treatment, would benefit from an air move rather than by surface transport. Priority four is for the patient whose movement by air is more a matter of convenience rather than a medical requirement.

As for classifications, these take into account immobile or sitting patients, psychiatric patients and what are known as non-entitled patients. The last are borderline cases, some of whom may or may not be helped by the RAF aeromedical organization. These cases will only be accepted for air transportation if there is official approval. There are other criteria such as it being clinically essential the patient be moved by air, that it cannot be done by a civil airline and that space and payload are available. Normally the sponsor or the patient himself will be required to pay charges, though these may be waived if the non-entitled patient is in great hardship — as in the case of the hostages.

Before any patient, entitled or non-entitled, receives aeromedical services, much goes on in the background by way of signals. These have order of precedence (Flash, Immediate, Priority and Routine). They are dated and timed to within minutes past the hour stated. Messages are identified by subject indicator codes and all locations involved fully identified. The subject matter occupies the first line of the message text. As for the message itself, the official dictate, which every communicator should follow, is that 'the message must be brief, consistent with clarity, and unambiguous.'

Assuming the signals result in approval for aeromedical action, the RAF medical officer delegated to initiate arrangements has a clear set of responsibilities. First and foremost he must advise on the aeromedical aspect. He has then to arrange for suitable in-flight facilities, provide loading and unloading aids, see to the medical equipment required for the patient's journey and condition. The RAF likes to have all such patients, where possible, admitted to a medical Unit on the day prior to the flight. This is so they can receive a thorough pre-flight examination and briefing — dependent on the patient's condition.

A typical aeromedical briefing will begin with the person who is to accompany the patient introducing himself. It is an important part of the procedure as RAF doctors and medical assistants are often dressed in flying suits or even combat-type clothing. The patient should then be told about the flight, the times of take-off and landing including any stop-overs, the make of aircraft and flight procedures, also about transport at the deplaning airfield. It is likewise important to find out if the patient has ever had any problems with previous flights or indeed anxieties about flying. The patient has to be reassured that he is in safe hands, that his luggage and personal effects will be cared for, also all documents such as identification card, passport and other necessary papers are in order.

Patients will be allocated seats or stretchers and they must not exchange these without permission of an aeromedical team member. Aeromed personnel are responsible for every aspect of their patients' welfare and safety. They are also trained in the equipment available in that aircraft, as will be presently outlined. There are many rules laid down for the handling of patients before and after they are emplaned. To take but a few — all stretcher supports, clamps and stanchions must be properly arranged and secured, all aeromedical gear should be correctly stowed leaving no insecure articles, and there must be sufficient life jackets to hand.

Patients are brought aboard before non-medical passengers, but will deplane on the instructions of the medical team. In-flight feeding facilities are not normally provided for short range journeys, but are available from the cabin catering staff on long ones at the discretion of the aeromedical officer. In practice, the aircraft stewards look after their passengers and the aeromedical people their patients. Mothers with babies are expected to feed and look after their infants themselves, though cabin and medical staff will help if necessary. At the other end of the life span, a death during flight is usually reported when the plane reaches UK air space or, if that is impracticable, a diversion may be made to a military airfield. The registration of a death in the air is the responsibility of the captain, who is the official informant.

Aeromedics are trained to regard the aircraft as a flying ward and, although the flight may be of relatively short duration, they have to know the precise location of their patients and all associated equipment. To this end a loading plan is prepared 24 hours before the scheduled departure of the aircraft for use by ground handling medical staff, air movements passenger staff, the aircraft's loadmaster and, of course, by the accompanying aeromedical team. The diagnosis of the patient is the prime factor used to determine his or her whereabouts on the plane. This diagnosis, however, is not recorded on patient loading plans used by non-medical staff.

Comprehensive guidelines are laid down for the handling of stretcher and walking patients. Usually, stretcher patients are placed head first with their feet aft. Patients needing the most nursing care are put in the most easily accessible position. Walking patients are given inside or centre seats with the medical escort having the outside one. Patients with leg plasters are allocated seats with sufficient room for the limb to be raised and supported. Patients accompanied by a family are, wherever possible, seated together.

On a plane carrying patients the stretcher compartment is out of bounds to all other walking patients and other passengers. This compartment or area is usually curtained off and everyone in the vicinity gives due regard to the patient(s) on board. In fact the flight stage is usually the swiftest and smoothest part of a patient's journey. What is more essential for aeromedical moves are ground handling services available at the emplaning, intermediate and destination airfields.

Together, the aeromedical and air movements staff have to ensure that the correct equipment is ready and waiting to get the patient(s) on and off that type of aircraft. There are many ways this can be achieved — by truck and trolley, forklift and pallet or by scissor-lift vehicles. Walking patients may require special steps or ramps.

On many routes flown by RAF aircraft in the aeromedical role, there may be the need to stop over at certain airfields. Most walking patients can deplane and be supervised by the medical team in the appropriate arrival or departure lounges, whereas stretcher cases usually remain on the plane. Care must therefore be provided for the patient(s) on the aircraft. When refuelling takes place during such a stop, the aircraft has to be parked on a heading thus allowing wind to carry fumes away from

Above Aeromedics receive a rescued patient from a helicopter.

Above left Sea rescue by helicopter.

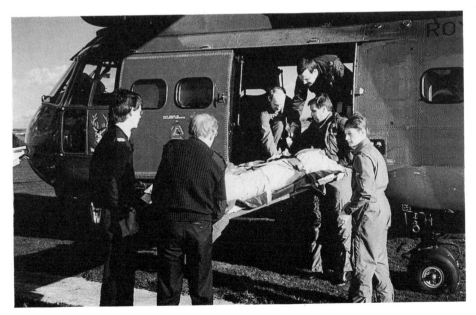

Removal of a stretcher case from a helicopter.

the main exit door in use. Further to all the precautions taken during refuelling the aeromedical team has to remain with and monitor the well-being of the patient.

A considerable amount of equipment, both aeromedical and general, is required when moving every patient. The listed items range from medical bags carried on the aircraft and by the in-flight escort to oxygen cylinders, regulators and masks, drip stands, bed pans and disposable urinal bottles. Medical bags contain various drugs as required, and there are what are known as 'comfy bags' with pyjamas, towels, soap, toothbrush and toothpaste, face flannel and talcum powder. The airfield or hospital that emplanes the patient is usually responsible for supplying the stretcher on which there are a mattress; two sheets, pillows and pillow slips; three blankets and a safety harness.

The items to be carried may seem self-evident, but the RAF has discovered from

A VC10 cabin stripped out before installation of aeromedical fittings.

long experience that checks and double checks are necessary to ensure successful operations. All equipment has to be tested for serviceability before being sent on aeromedical tasks. It would be very embarrassing, as well as thoroughly unprofessional, to take equipment on an aircraft to do a specific task, then be unable to carry out that task due to faults or missing items. Another important point is to ensure the complete aeromedical equipment is accompanied by the correct documentation. Without it the captain and loadmaster could treat the package as suspicious. There is already so much to be done before an aircraft leaves the ground that unnecessary delays must be eliminated. Moreover, certain items of aeromedical equipment — e.g. oxygen cylinders, batteries and chemicals — are classified as dangerous air cargo, therefore identification, packing and handling are extremely important.

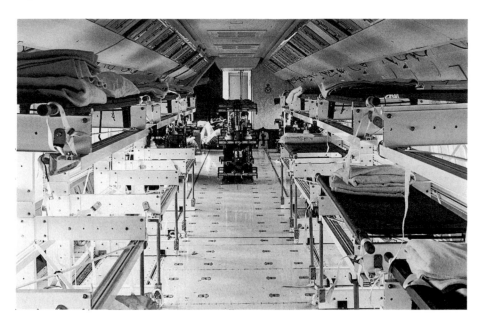

A similar cabin fully fitted with stretcher frames and oxygen equipment.

Another aspect of aeromedical work is concerned with knowing the aircraft on which the patient will be carried — particularly its layout, facilities, systems and safety equipment. Most aeromedical work carried out by the RAF is done in the VC10s and TriStars at Brize Norton. These are big planes containing a considerable amount of equipment with which the aeromedic must be familiar and be able to use on behalf of his patient if called upon to do so.

Regarding the VC10, its main cabin can accommodate up to a maximum of 78 stretcher cases with seating for medical staff. This maximum is seldom required and, in any case, it would be necessary to remove some normally fixed fittings to achieve total capacity. The more usual role is for up to three stretcher cases. These are provided for by a pair of stretcher posts permanently stowed in the forward lower cargo hold. Once the two posts are installed in the cabin, then three stretchers can be supported one above the other. The stretchers used are standard ambulance ones each equipped with a pillow and sheets, also a harness to secure patients. Apart from securing the patient safely to the stretcher, the harness serves to prevent aggravation of any injuries during loading and flight. Quick-release fittings are used on all such harnesses.

The siting of stretchers, oxygen and medical equipment is but part of the knowledge that aeromedics must have about the aircraft in which they and their patients are flying. The VC10 (as does the TriStar — to be covered later) has a set of emergency equipment items, some visible and others contained in racks, recesses and lockers. The aeromedic who is responsible for his patient(s) must know the whereabouts of the VC10's eight emergency exits, four escape chutes and ten escape ropes; the fire extinguishers and smoke masks; life jackets and rafts; first aid kits and survival packs. As previously mentioned, the flight crew is responsible for the aircraft, the cabin crew for the passengers and the aeromedical people for their patients.

The TriStar is an even larger aircraft with, correspondingly, more handling and safety equipment for the aeromedics to master. The two versions at Brize Norton — the C2 all-passenger TriStar and the KC1 passenger/freighter — require different stretcher handling arrangements. With the C2, access for stretcher patients is through the starboard side passenger door. With the KC1 there is the large upward opening

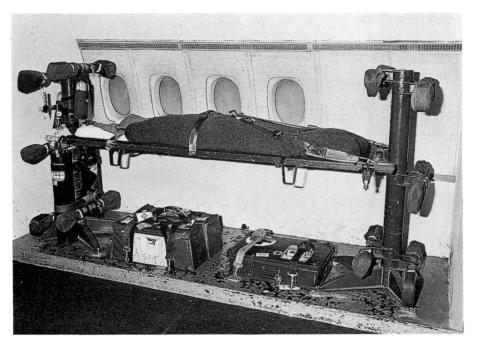

Stretcher and medical kit on a pallet platform.

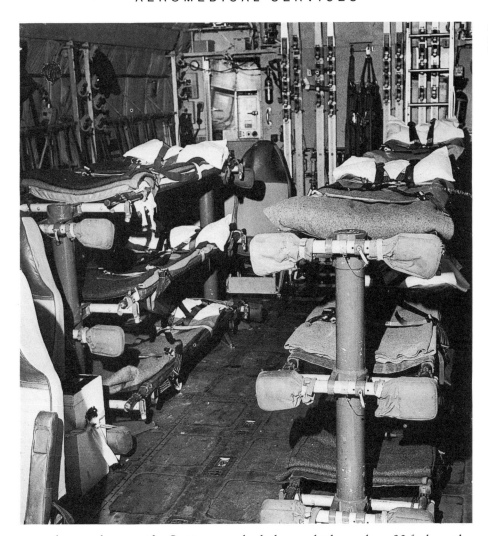

A high density three-tier stretcher system fitted in a VC10 cabin.

cargo door on the port side. Getting up to both doors, which are about 20 ft above the ground, is a vital matter when one is dealing with patients on stretchers. Such cases are put aboard and taken off TriStar aircraft by means of an in-flight catering vehicle. This has a platform which can be raised from near ground to cabin floor level. Four stabilizing legs on the chassis assist in smoothing the transfer.

The TriStar C2s can take four stretchers as standard plus two more if required. This aircraft version has an area where the seats and a bulkhead have been removed for aeromedical purposes. In the case of the KC1s, the floor of the fuselage has been fitted to take a roll-on/off pallet system. The system provides great flexibility in installing passenger seats, kitchen units, freight packs and stretcher equipment. This in turn allows swift and varied role changes for the aircraft. With the KC1, up to 72 patients on stretchers and 28 aeromedics in nearby seats can be accommodated. There is also the TriStar K1 version (halfway between the all-passenger C1 and the fully-palletized KC1) which can take 62 stretchers and 17 aeromedics when converted to that role.

These — the RAF Brize Norton VC10 and TriStar aircraft together with aeromedical teams — therefore combine to fulfil an inspiring as well as a necessary range of humanitarian services. No two examples are the same, apart from the overriding objective of caring for patients and often saving their lives. The following

Above A non-infectious patient in an aircraft sick bay. Note the passengers in the background.

Above right A patient's view of a waiting ambulance on aircraft arrival at RAF Brize Norton.

aeromedical stories are typical of war and peacetime operations.

During the Falklands war, aeromedical teams operated in and around Dakar, Ascension Island and Port Stanley. They collected, cared for and brought home many patients by the quickest possible means — using aircraft and their aeromedical skills. Strangely enough, the episode which appears to have lingered in the aeromedics' minds is that of collecting Falklands patients from a nearby neutral country. To the Brize aircrew and aeromedical team, their first surprise was on landing and being parked next to an Argentinian plane. 'There we were,' the tale went, 'wing tip to wing tip with the enemy.' To prevent any incident on neutral soil, the country concerned laid on guards armed with machine guns and machetes, also with leash-straining Alsatian dogs. Every movement of RAF personnel was under such escorts. However, the object of the exercise was to receive British Service patients off a hospital ship and fly them home. There were 17 patients, the neutral country laid on 17 ambulances from dock to airport and, within 24 hours, all the patients were back in Britain.

The following two examples cover routine aeromedical duties, the second of which turned into an emergency. Each week an RAF aircraft flies aeromedical staff to Germany for the purpose of assessing and possibly returning British Service patients to the UK. The medics go to various German hospitals where there are British patients, and to British military hospitals throughout Germany. The cases vary from car and other accidents to serious illnesses. The assessment of each case involves the patient's condition, treatment and ability to travel by air. It also requires the preparation of transfer documentation and the dispensing, if necessary, of drugs. An RAF Andover aircraft of 60 Squadron is usually provided for the service as it is very versatile, taking up to 15 stretcher/walking patients. In most cases the aircraft will touch down at Northolt which is handy for Service hospitals at Halton, Woolwich and Aldershot. This routine alone shows how well the Services look after their own.

In the case of the routine transfer which became an emergency, a Service patient with a suspected brain tumour had to be brought home from Cyprus. The aeromedical team which went to fetch him included a doctor (an anaesthetist). The flight from Akrotiri to Brize Norton was uneventful and the patient apparently stable — until the last half-hour when his condition began to deteriorate rapidly. At the precise moment of the aircraft wheels touching Brize runway, the patient stopped breathing. Immediately the aeromedical team set about resuscitating him and putting him on a special ventilator they had brought with them. This took place while the aircraft was taxiing. It came to a stop beside the ambulance which took the patient and medics to the John Radcliffe Hospital in nearby Oxford. Three weeks later that person was back at work.

Another, altogether different aeromedical effort took place during the writing of this book. One assistant was part-interviewed on a Tuesday and a second appointment made for the Friday. The concluding interview had to be postponed to the beginning of the following week because the aeromedical assistant had been sent to Barbados. When eventually asked what occurred, he mentioned having to bring back two injured sailors.

What had happened was this. A Royal Navy vessel had called into Georgetown, Guyana. There a friendly football match was played, but it unfortunately resulted in one sailor badly hurting his back during a fall and another breaking his arm. The Naval doctor treated both sailors while the ship sailed to Port of Spain, Trinidad and advised aerial repatriation to the United Kingdom. The aeromedical assessment was that, while both patients could walk, they needed assistance.

Shortly after the message was received at Brize Norton, the RAF Flight Nursing Attendant travelled to Gatwick and boarded a British Airways flight leaving for Bridgetown, Barbados. From Bridgetown he caught an island hopping plane (Barbados—St Vincent—Grenada—Trinidad). At Port-of-Spain the British High Commissioner had reserved seats for the two RN sailors and the RAF aeromedic back to Gatwick. There the incoming flight was met by a Navy ambulance and the Brize attendant accompanied his charges to Haslar Hospital, Portsmouth. The series of journeys and the responsibilities involved would leave an average person exhausted. 'No problem,' said the aeromedical assistant, and went on where he had left off a week ago.

But, of course, there are problems which can only be tackled by constant training and acquired expertise. The Gulf War presented many examples of RAF aeromedical professionalism. One of the tasks allocated to the Brize team was the recovery of those air crew and Special Services personnel who had fallen into the hands of the enemy.

The call came through at short notice on a Sunday afternoon. The Iraqis were prepared to release British prisoners, and an aeromedical team of eight, including three psychiatrists, was to leave as soon as possible. By early evening a Brize VC10 with the aeromedics aboard had left on the six hour flight to Bahrain. Early next morning, after an overnight stop, the plane and team continued to Amman where the POWs were to be released. What did the medical people expect and encounter?

'Malnutrition, infestation, untreated injuries,' came the bleak reply, 'but most of all the dangers from post-traumatic stress disorders.' The RAF medical team provided surface treatment while beginning to build in-depth psychological profiles of each individual returned to them. Once assessed, it was explained, this helps the patient to start readjusting. Treatment began on the aircraft. It meant creating a friendly and relaxing environment that is often helped by taking along a relative or colleague of the patient. Telling the story, perhaps again and again, assists in getting it out of the system.

Over the space of a week, the Iraqis released 12 British prisoners. Each was met, treated and flown back to the United Kingdom as soon as possible. This example alone sums up the RAF's Aeromedical Services. They are at every stressful and traumatic occasion involving Service personnel and the use of aircraft, but prefer to keep in the background. That is why this chapter has been included about them.

Chapter 10

VIP TREATMENT

From time to time in this book, references have been made to the VIP work at RAF Brize Norton. It is a high profile subject which sometimes tends to exclude everything else done by a very active Station. 'Oh Brize,' people remark, 'that is where they look after the VIPs.' The simplification needs expanding and qualifying. Certainly Brize Norton does provide air transport for important people. As has been described, it also does so for thousands of people, for passengers of all ranks, Services and civilians. The main flying roles of the Station are to provide such strategic air transport services and to operate Squadrons of aircraft equipped to carry out air-to-air refuelling anywhere in the world. The official handbook about RAF Brize Norton puts the VIP part of Station activities in its rightful place. It adds that 'Aeromedical flights, special VIP and military exercise flights are undertaken as required.'

'As required', however, should not be regarded as an odd job fitted in somehow when the Station is not too busy. It is a task which the RAF takes very seriously and, to repeat a word used in the opening sentence of this Chapter, it entails 'work' — a lot of hard work on the part of many Brize people. Before going on to what is actually involved — the extra duties, responsibilities and deadlines — it is necessary to define the VIP acronym a little further. Some say it started to be used in World War II when RAF operations had to include the likes of Winston Churchill, senior officers and high level government officials. Others claim it began during the early post-war days when separate aircraft lounges and parts of passenger cabins were set aside for more important individuals. Be this as it may, there are graduations in every society and how RAF Brize Norton hosts them is the subject of this chapter.

The fact of the matter is that RAF Brize Norton hosts VIPs almost on a daily basis, year in and year out. A glance at the passenger lists will show Lords, knights, admirals, generals and air marshals among the commanders and lieutenants, the Sergeants and rankers, often all together with their wives and children. So the handling of these passengers, going about their various duties, is a normal part of Brize's activities. Some are singled out for a brief greeting, an extra drink, a better seat. Others simply blend into the main proceedings of moving up to 200 passengers aboard an aircraft, then getting that aircraft to somewhere in Europe, the Mediterranean or North America. This day-to-day handling of VIPs by Brize Norton has to be understood.

Nevertheless, the scale of VIPs dealt with by RAF Brize Norton does go higher, to the highest in the land. Climbing up the scale beyond Air Officer level, its equivalent among other Services, and government officials, the next stages are those of cabinet ministers, in particular the Foreign Secretary and Prime Minister who regularly use Brize aircraft. To deal with such situations, it is necessary to modify aircraft interiors. These are called 'Fits' and their configurations will be determined by the Ministry of Defence.

RAF Brize Norton does the honours.

The idea and the implementation of 'Fits' may seem curious, but adaptations are directly linked to practical requirements. For example, when a senior minister travels, he or she (a) has a certain amount of staff, (b) needs to keep in touch with unfolding events and (c) is often accompanied by members of the media. It would be totally impractical to put this mix on to an aircraft of standard fit and hope they will sort themselves out. The different 'fits', as will be described, are not so much luxurious as practical. A cabinet minister has to work or rest. His staff must be able to communicate and advise. The media require facilities and opportunities to interview and report. The flight crew and cabin crew have their responsibilities to aircraft and passengers. Taken in this context, the air transportation of a Prime Minister follows the same practical pattern as conveying a senior aircraftman to a new posting.

Official cars awaiting VIP visitors.

The world's Press unpacking to record VIP passenger arrival.

Referring to the scale of treatment previously mentioned, the highest for VIPs is Fit 1. There is, however, what could be called a super-scale, that of a State Visit which in turn requires a State Fit. The Monarch and the Royal Family travel in many ways, some formal and others so unobtrusive that no notice is given or taken. However, for a State Visit, the responsibility of air transporting one's Sovereign becomes a formidable undertaking. Various Brize people, interviewed in the course of writing this book, put it in different ways such as: 'It is an honour' or 'It entails a great deal of preparatory work.' The most memorable remark was: 'For a VIP flight everything should be perfect. When we carry Her Majesty the Queen, everything must be more than perfect.'

VIP and State flights (the latter are often referred to as VVIPs) usually start with a

Media people with cameras at the ready crowd into Brize Norton Passenger Terminal.

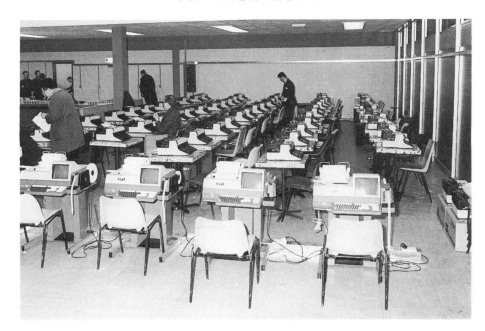

A Press Centre set up to help the media.

phone call a month beforehand. A Prime Ministerial visit is being planned to the Gulf States or Her Majesty has to visit certain Commonwealth countries. This alerting call is followed by more details. The Operations Staff, together with the Engineering Wing and usually No.10 Squadron at Brize Norton begin to 'juggle' aircraft. This is a complicated task because the VC10s involved are already committed to scheduled training and other flights as well as to maintenance work owing to their inexorable stages of serviceability. Regarding the last mentioned factor, the engineers, immediately upon hearing about a VIP or VVIP flight, begin studying each aircraft's technical history for the last five years. All concerned have to work out what should be done and how to do it in the timescale allowed. Their thoughts and deliberations then have to be set down on paper and sent to London for approval.

A corner of the Press Centre with self-service catering.

Television cameras on the roof of the Passenger Terminal. Brize Norton provides every facility linked with strict security.

The 'fit' proposed has to meet the circumstances for that flight. Conditions of communications, security, special equipment, accommodation, catering, departures and arrivals, emplaning and deplaning — all must be planned and agreed before being put into operation.

Taking the highest level — a State or VVIP flight — as an example, the two best VC10s at RAF Brize Norton are earmarked as primary and back-up aircraft. The RAF always has a back-up in case something unforeseen happens with the primary. In any case, many State flights involve two aircraft. The first will carry the Sovereign, escorts and small personal staff. The second will convey the regalia, senior diplomats and staff officers necessary on these prestige occasions.

The two aircraft, primary and back-up, are 'eased out' of regular operations so that the work plans for them can be put into effect. To start with, both aircraft receive a full service irrespective of what may have recently transpired. Moreover, every system component that has exceeded 50% of its operating life is changed for a new one. What this means in engineering terms is that each fresh component has now to be tested and proven. It means bay testing, ground testing on the aircraft, then flight testing so that performance meets all specifications. Flight testing is especially important because what might have done well in the workbay or just outside the hangar may show reluctance at the -60oC of 30,000 ft. An experienced pilot summed up the situation when he said: 'A climb through heavy rain to a deep freeze atmosphere soon proves the best components.'

While the prime and back-up aircraft are being prepared by the engineers, the Squadron is also selecting the air and ground crews who will fly in them. All agree that for a State flight the responsibility can only be shouldered by the best personnel available. Aircraft, as compared to land vehicles and sea vessels, carry extra hazards that may need the most experienced of pilots and other crew members to overcome them. When the Monarch flies with the Royal Air Force the crew of the aircraft, chosen for this honour is increased and in some areas doubled. There will be two captains, one co-pilot, two Loadmasters, three stewards and two ground engineers carried, together with protocol and escort officers as well as four guards. There are two reasons for the duplication on the piloting side. First, as will be explained in the next paragraph, a great deal of extra work is required on such trips. Having two captains

HM Queen Elizabeth and HRH Prince Philip meet Brize families.

and one co-pilot thus ensures that the heavy demands are met without overstretching crew members. Secondly, should any member become ill or meet with an accident, the task can continue as planned because the reserve was there from the start.

With regard to the extra work, consider the situation of the aircraft captain. Full responsibility rests with him. If anything untoward happens his colleagues, the Air Force, his country and the world will know that he was the person who made the mistake. All his training, dedication and indeed loyalty can be called into question in a split second. The inherent problems go far beyond those of a normal flight. He can be called upon to fly into places neither he nor the rest of his crew have ever visited. He is confronted with much increased problems in pre-flight planning.

A Brize captain, experienced with these special flights, tried to explain. 'It is an axiom of aviation that a pilot should spend two hours on the ground for every hour in

HM the Queen views a display put on by the Brize Norton based Aeromedical Centre.

the air. He must think ahead and plan for every contingency. For a routine flight, which we may do weekly, there is up to five hours planning by the pilots and navigator. When a VIP or VVIP flight is involved, the planning time increases to four or five times that of normal. A State visit to Montreal, Delhi or Sydney is fraught with side issues, apart from the main flight from A to B. A stop for refuelling means moving the whole hierarchy out of and back on to the plane. A great deal goes on in advance, clearing and protecting airspace. Perhaps the most difficult problem is arriving not only on time but to the second.'

'Arriving on time,' another captain said, 'is one of the main problems. Our pilots and navigators go into much planning and fine detail to ensure this. On the one hand, it is no use arriving half an hour early while the president of the country being visited is still driving to the airport. On the other hand, he cannot stand for half an hour at his end of the red carpet while the aircraft captain tries to unravel air traffic or taxi patterns. We work on a sequence of time marks, making up and losing split seconds, as we touch down, taxi and finally halt the aircraft so that the exit door lines up with that carpet.'

This combination of circumstances, of distances and timings, are multiplied when several VIPs flights are made in one day. The schedule of a busy Foreign or Defence Secretary — himself tackling another combination of circumstances — puts great demands on the aircraft crews. During a crisis such as the recent Middle East one, shuttle diplomacy demanded fully serviceable planes and ever versatile crews. One pilot recalls a minister on his way back from India having to stop at a Gulf State for a discussion with its rulers. The discussion was prolonged, but the minister still had to be back at London Airport at a certain hour. The pilot was faced with over an hour to make up on an eight hour journey.

The Golden Rule of VIP flying is apparently to treat all circumstances as normal, all problems as soluble. The VIP plane becomes a government department on the move. The minister may well have a staff of 10-15 with him, permanent secretaries and undersecretaries, stenographers and personal assistants. During the flight many messages arrive and are sent. The affairs of State do not cease at 30,000 ft over the Atlantic or the Alps. And there is another aspect in that further aft there may be several media people following the minister's every move, hoping to interview him or at least to receive a few quotable words. In the case of television, the reporters are accompanied by camera and sound staff. Together with their equipment they can easily jam up the confines of any aircraft, even a wide-bodied one. The aircraft Loadmaster and stewards must maintain firm if friendly control.

The aircrews and ground crews at RAF Brize Norton are very discreet on details of their VIP flights — which is as it should be. Their main concern seems to be getting it right. These important flights concentrate minds wonderfully and, as one Sergeant put it: 'Everyone has to contribute. We have to be a well-functioning team, always working together, or we would fail.' True teamwork results in the kind of efficiency which seems almost casual and effortless. Its practitioners, moving around quietly and smiling constantly, appear to blend into the background to the point of invisibility. So when the RAF aircraft arrives with Her Majesty the Queen, the Prime Minister, a war hero or a released hostage, the plane and crew are hardly noticed.

The preparation of aircraft for VIP flying includes an important stage which should now be described. It must again be emphasized that the VC10s at RAF Brize Norton are working planes. They will have been carrying passengers and freight, troops and armaments, to desert airfields and other remote places during the weeks prior to their selection for VIP usage. The external paintwork may be in poor condition. The interior trim in particular takes a hammering from boots, boxes, tool kits and all the other awkward articles which are part and parcel of Service life. The eventual workaday state of the plane is certainly not a sight to be seen by a Queen or a Prime Minister, or by those at the receiving airports.

So, after the aircraft has been taken out of service and after the technical assessments, component replacements and thorough testing, the plane requires transformation to pristine condition. Externally it is examined inch by inch, rivet by rivet from its nose to the tip of the tall tail. Every scratch and blemish is noted for cleaning, polishing and painting. Often, if the aircraft has been operating in tough terrain, such as deserts, a complete paint job may be necessary. This is done away from Brize Norton by specialist contractors to RAF colour specification and finish.

The next step is to remove everything within the aircraft cabin from behind the flight deck right through to the rear bulkhead. Seats and kitchen units, bulkheads and cabin wall trim all go, to leave a bare metal interior. During this removal operation,

Above Preparing the outside of a VC10 aircraft for a State flight. Every inch outside and inside is meticulously inspected.

Below Brize Norton Role Equipment team members laying carpet partly up the cabin wall.

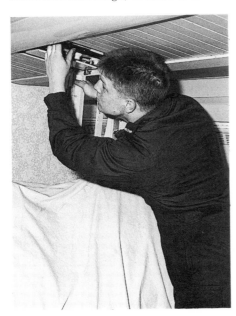

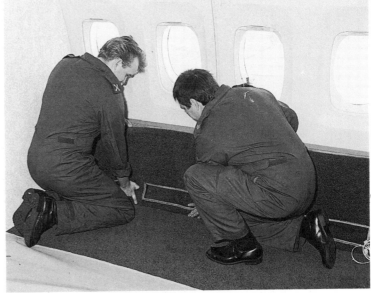

opportunity is taken to inspect the interior of the fuselage frame and the normally concealed services. Frayed leads and loose ductings are made good and the whole stripped down interior is thoroughly cleaned.

It is at this stage that another specialist section comes into its own. This section looks after visiting aircraft and role equipment. Normally it is responsible for adapting the VC10 aircraft operated by No.10 Squadron to fulfil different roles. There are 16 different styles and standards, 11 of which are working ones and five for VIPs up to the State Visit role previously mentioned. One week the aircraft may carry only passengers, the next week a mix of people and freight or, in an emergency, stretchers. The role equipment team of about ten, all of whom are airframe technicians and mechanics, are called upon to effect these changes. They have a hangar full of role equipment near to the Base Hangar where the aircraft to be converted is taken. They mostly use a high-lift wagon for conveying and lifting articles into the waiting stripped-down VIP plane.

Regarding members of the role equipment team, their RAF training and experience is such that they can work on a range of other more technical tasks than carpet laying and curtain hanging. However, service means doing what has to be done and, in this case, they have to convert a bare metal tube into a place of quiet comfort; though not, as will be shown, one of any undue luxury. Team members usually carry out VIP duties for an interim period because, apart from being overtrained for such duties, each VIP refit has an inexorable deadline. The preliminary inspections, engineering work and tests have been known to stretch well towards the deadline, leaving the role equipment people less and less time to do their equally necessary duties. 'It is an interesting job,' one airframe technician said, 'but I wouldn't want to make a career of it.'

Their first task is to lay a gold coloured carpet. For a VVIP flight, the carpet runs from side to side and stem to stern. With VIP flights parts of the same carpet are used to cover various areas. With the latter the seat mounting tracks and other floor fittings can be seen. One doubts if they are noticed so far down under the seats, but there is this subtle built-in difference. Once the underlay and carpeting have been fixed using double-sided tape, the surface is covered by dust sheets and walk strips before the next stage is started.

The next stage entails fitting new or refurbished wall panels and bulkheads. As already stated, these take a hammering during everyday usage so they are returned to the role equipment hangar and VIP kits issued in their place. There are various styles and finishes of bulkheads, but basically these are boards cut to various shapes and covered in tasteful vinyls. Each bulkhead has attachments for floor fittings, and top retaining clips. With the gold coloured carpet, wall trim panels and bulkheads, the interior of the VIP plane starts to look just that.

For a VIP flight, the centre position of what was the passenger cabin is transformed by the bulkheads (and refinements still to come) into a private area. This means that the 'long tube' aircraft configuration is divided into three distinct zones. The nose section remains that of the flight deck which retains a kitchen unit and small rest area for the aircrew. Similarly the tail section is allocated to the Loadmaster, stewards, security police and ground crew. If members of the media are aboard they also find themselves in that part of the cabin. Those television pictures of an airborne minister talking to the Press generally take place in this vicinity.

The Role Equipment staff work to a plan and a series of lists. The plan is headed by the VIP Flight No., the type of fit required and the date when everything has either to be perfect or more than perfect. The plan also gives the name of the person responsible for its implementation. 'Therefore,' one Warrant Officer said, 'whatever happens, the work is always ready on time.' On time means a high level inspection — by no less than an Air Commodore in the case of the Monarch — so there are usually a series of pre-inspections by Flight Lieutenants, Squadron Leaders and all ranks upwards.

'What,' a newcomer will ask, 'does such a distinguished personage as the Queen or a Prince have in her or his section of aircraft?' One expects the ultimate in luxury, and is surprised to see quiet comfort, yes, supplemented by some privacy. Starting at the bulkhead behind the flight crews quarter, a heavy curtain signals that the Royal compartment lies beyond it. A steward usually lingers by the refreshment unit on one side of the curtain and an aide-de-camp on the other. Aft of the aide-de-camp is a further bulkhead and another set of heavy curtains. They open into a Royal living area the whole width of the cabin. The central walkway is maintained, but on one side (usually port) there are two chairs on each side of a table. The chairs are aircraft type though wider with generous reclining ability and foot rests. Across the central

Below left David Gower on a visit to RAF Brize Norton.

Below Exciting days. The breakthrough meeting between Prime Minister Thatcher and President Gorbachev at RAF Brize Norton.

John McCarthy arrives at Lyneham in a Brize VC10.

walkway there is a lounge area which contains a horseshoe-shaped divan together with a low coffee-type table.

Moving further aft from the Royal living quarter to the sleeping one, double curtains this time open to another room containing a divan bed on the port side and, on the starboard side, a dressing table area. More curtains can be pulled across the divan and dressing areas for privacy. The use of curtains continues as one moves aft

Jackie Mann also arriving at Lyneham in a Brize VC10.

Terry Waite gives a thumbs-up after his ordeal. With him *(left rear)* is Wing Commander David McDonnell, OC Operations Wing who headed the Brize Norton VC10 flight crew.

between the Royal wardrobes. A final set of curtains across the centre way leads into the aft part of the passenger cabin containing the Queen's personal staff. The impression that one receives from the whole suite — in fact the complete fit — is of neatness and good taste. The decor of furnishings, curtains and capets could be described as combining earth and autumn colours — shades of brown, beige and gold. Like the air and ground crew, it does not intrude. Yet this Royal suite retains essential aircraft items for all passengers alike — seat belts, overhead lights, air flow controls, oxygen masks and other emergency equipment.

After the decor come the details. They are set out in another list on the clipboard of the man in charge. Again this is headed by the Flight No. and Date/Time of Departure. Logically, for a State Visit, the list begins with flags. In addition to the Royal Ensign, the national flags of the countries being visited have to be included. Together with small flag poles, they need to be available and at hand for fitment during approach to the arrival point.

Flags and poles are only the first two items on a list which runs to three pages. The way to appreciate this attention to detail is to include some (though by no means all) of the items covered. They include:

Doormats	8	Rugs	1 per seat and 4 spares
Umbrellas	2	Pillows, small	1 per seat
Vacuum cleaner	1	Pillow slips	1 per pillow
Carpet sweeper	1	Clock set	1
Dustpan and brush	2	World map	1
Coat hangers	8 per rail	Squadron prints	1 set
Headrest covers	1 packet		

The list goes on, yet it is but one of many lists that the leaders of many teams are ensuring must be on that aircraft. There are lists of porcelain, silver, food and drinks, documents, spares, tools, communications equipment — all being checked and rechecked before arriving at the aircraft where every batch is checked again by the

Loadmaster and finally rechecked in situ. Strict control is also needed for personnel arriving with their different items — from an extra bottle of wine to a consignment of sheets and pillowslips. Despite its transformation, the aircraft cabin remains a long tube and can easily become blocked by personnel intent on completing their particular task.

The Royal role fit has been described in some detail. How does it differ from that of a government minister? Basically, ministerial planes follow the same concept of using the centre section, but they are more like flying offices. There is a communications section through which messages arrive and are sent during flight. There are sections for secretaries — called stenographers or plain typists — to distinguish them from undersecretaries and permanent secretaries. These sections are individually curtained and utilized as one would a series of offices. The work flow is forward from the communications and stenographers sections to the front section where the minister makes his deliberations. A nearby area with a divan is included to rest the ministerial head. Again the impression is not one of luxury, but rather that of a well-functioning commercial organization.

The night before the VIP aircraft is due for its final inspection and departure can be one of intense pressures. The lists of items already inspected and found wanting have yet to shrink to zero. Lights burn in the hangar, in the aircraft, in nearby bays and offices. Loadmasters frown over figures. Pilots and navigators go over alternatives. There is much cleaning and polishing. Those who make up the VIP crew, fore and aft, see to their best uniforms. Even flying suits, overalls and dust coats have to look like No.1 dress. One VIP crew member summed up the atmosphere as 'purposeful panic'.

The late night is succeeded by an early start. The assembly, the briefing, the attendance of each crew member to his or her duty comes almost as a relief after all the preparations. To the general public living in and around the airfield, the VIP aircraft taking off looks like just another Brize plane. Soon after that take-off the aircraft will have touched down again — perhaps at Heathrow to await a limousine bearing the Royal Ensign. Hours later the same aircraft may be seen coming to a stop between a reception stand and a guard of honour. The reception party, onlookers and television viewers will hardly give that aircraft a glance let alone begin to know the work that went into it — which is a good reason for including this Chapter.

Chapter 11
BRIZE PEOPLE

During a period of several months gathering material for this book dozens of people were interviewed. Those featured in the following pages are intended to show the diversity of Service life at RAF Brize Norton. Unfortunately there is not enough space to cover everyone.

Donna Trask

In the large and corporate body of the Royal Air Force, there are those known as auxiliaries. During normal times they either help out with humble yet helpful tasks or they are on standby at home. When an emergency arises the Air Force knows that it can rely on its auxiliaries — full time. They are trained and they are ready. They will take on any duty allocated to them, especially those that free the regulars for more forward operations. Such a person is Donna Trask and she exemplifies all those auxiliaries helping out or standing by at Brize Norton.

When interviewed, Donna Trask was employed at the Station's Personnel Services

Below left Donna Trask worked during the week as a civilian administration officer, and over most weekends trained with No.4624 (County of Oxford) Movements Squadron, Royal Auxiliary Air Force.

Below When Operation Granby occurred, Donna Trask was mobilized as a uniformed senior aircraftwoman.

flight, but due to go on maternity leave. During the week she worked as a civilian administrative officer, and over most weekends trained with No.4624 (County of Oxford) Movements Squadron. The minimum attendance requirements are one evening a week, one weekend a month and 15 continuous days each year. Donna's husband is a Sergeant in Air Movements, so it is a shared activity. Donna's brother is also in the RAF as a Sergeant air Loadmaster on helicopters. Thus the background is a Service one — what she called 'an Air Forcey family'.

Donna grew up in Bath where she was educated at the well-known Ralph Allen School. From the moment she left School Donna wanted to join the Air Force, but every trade she tried was closed at the time. During this period Donna could be said to be engaged in tri-Service activities. She worked for the Navy in Bath, joined the RAF's No.93 ATC Squadron, did a parachute jump with the Army and was presented with her gold Duke of Edinburgh Award by Prince Philip himself. The RAF won in the end. Donna married Hugh Trask in March 1989, then moved to Brize Norton in October of the same year.

The move gave Donna the opportunity to join No.4624 — the largest auxiliary Squadron in the RAF. Living nearby in married quarters, she could keep up her training and be ready to respond should a state of emergency arise. Meanwhile Donna worked as a local purchasing officer in the Station's Supply Wing and thoroughly enjoyed it. 'My duties,' she explained, 'ranged from supplying a handful of nails to ordering a complete aircraft windscreen. Like the Supply Wing, I dealt either through the MOD or direct with companies. It was a matter of knowing the procedures and especially of being able to act quickly. Every job was different and I enjoyed them all.' What type of aircraft windscreen was it and how much did it cost? Promptly Donna answered: 'TriStar £24,000.'

During this idyllic period of nails and windscreens the Desert Storm blew up. Donna Trask was mobilized as a uniformed senior aircraftwoman. No.4624 Squadron came up to full strength and its members were sent to different bases including RAF Wildenrath, Germany; Lyneham, Wiltshire and Brize Norton, Oxfordshire. While remaining at Brize, Donna now faced — like everyone else there — a formidable war workload. In theory she had to work three days and three nights on duty followed by

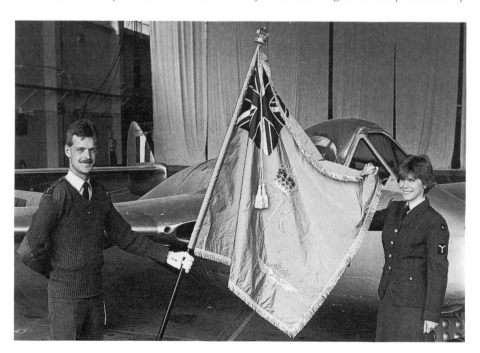

Donna Trask with the Sovereign's Colour which HM the Queen presented to No.4624 Movements Squadron, Royal Auxiliary Air Force, based at Brize Norton.

three off. In practice she was working 12 hours a day then 13 hours a night with only meal times as a break.

Moreover, it was more physical work than paper work. Slightly built Donna was placed on a Movements Traffic team which meant loading and unloading, as if forever. Her team had handling aids — fork lifts, baggage conveyors, Land Rovers and Noddy trucks pulling trolleys. Each team member was trained to use all such equipment, but at the end of a shift everyone's muscles ached. In Donna's case she kept this up from January to April whilst her husband, as a regular Air Movements Sergeant at No.4624 Squadron, was busy training new recruits in case of further mobilization. At that time they seemed to pass like ships in the night, but it was necessary and both accepted this.

At the beginning of April 1991 Donna was sent to RAF Wildenrath where help was needed 'topping up' aircraft returning from the Gulf. To the general public, the war might seem to be over, though for Service personnel it was a particularly busy period. Donna returned to Brize Norton towards the end of April and was demobilized two weeks later. During call up she had passed a Promotion Board and, on her return, relocated to the Personnel Services flight beside Admin Headquarters. Her new duties included processing travel claims and particularly helping parents with children at Service Schools. Meanwhile, Donna's husband Hugh had become Senior NCO i/c Examinations for No.4626 Squadron, setting and marking up to 180 examination test papers. From the foregoing it might seem that the Trasks are so Service-minded as to exclude everything else. But no, at the time of being interviewed, Donna was primarily interested in approaching motherhood. As for hobbies, these are drawing and reading — the latter in some depth — also horse care and management evening classes at college. 'Hopefully,' Donna says, 'I shall be putting these to some use in a career with horses at a later stage.'

Graham Banks

The transporting of patients and casualties by air is a task the RAF does so expertly and smoothly that one almost ceases to notice it. However, like all smooth-running

Below left Graham Banks of Brize Norton's Aeromedical Training Centre which serves Army, Navy and Air Force personnel.

Below Graham Banks in field gear with a convoy of vehicles used by the aeromedical team.

operations, it is a case of training and practice make perfect. Yet another part of RAF Brize Norton's multi-faceted organization is the Aeromedical Evacuation Training Centre (AETC) serving Army, Navy and Air Force personnel. What AETC does was covered in Chapter 9, while this profile of Flight Sergeant Graham Banks is an attempt to show the career structure of a typical flight nursing attendant.

Like other people in these profiles, the Banks family has a Service background. Graham's father was an RAF medic for 22 years, and his mother a registered nurse. Similarly the family had to travel for Service postings and Graham's childhood included several overseas spells as far afield as Singapore and around the Far East. Latterly his education was at a secondary modern school in Wendover, then came the important career choice. Graham thought about nursing or farm management and, perhaps inevitably, applied for RAF aeromedical training.

He joined the Air Force in August 1976 and went to Swinderby for six weeks' basic training. That was followed by 4½ months at the Halton Institute of Community and Occupational Medicine. Halton is the main training centre for RAF medics, providing all aspects of theoretical and practical instruction. Following his RAF basic and medical training, Graham Banks went to the Station Medical Centre at RAF Honington in Suffolk from January 1977 to December 1979. There he had to work in and learn about many medical requirements such as dispensing, first aid and ambulance duties. His initial spell at Brize Norton was early in 1980 when he went on a pre-employment aeromedic course.

Trainees on this course include FNOs, who are commissioned flying nursing officers, and FNAs, non-commissioned flying nursing assistants, specializing in medical duties involving aircraft. For example, if a sick or wounded soldier has to be returned from Central America to Aldershot or a sailor from the South Atlantic to Portsmouth, RAF aeromedics will arrange and handle every detail of the operation. The soldier/sailor will be personally looked after until handed over to the proper authorities at the agreed destination. RAF medical staff accompanying patients have to learn a great deal about aircraft — their emergency equipment and particularly the supply systems such as oxygen. There are, of course, Loadmasters and stewards aboard, but they are themselves looking after passengers while the aeromedic must see to the patient(s).

From early 1980 to mid-1982 Graham was involved in a series of aeromedical duties, including the evacuation of casualties from the Falklands campaign. He made three trips to Montevideo in Uruguay and two to Stanley itself. These were interspersed with detachments to Ascension Island working with Hercules from Lyneham and VC10s from Brize Norton. That involved a lot of serious cases in difficult conditions. Following his South Atlantic stint, Graham was posted to a Support Unit in Germany as medic to British Service personnel and their families. He was there for three years and, in addition to dealing with the Brits, had to work with the US Air Force and local authorities. In order to facilitate the last, he learned to speak German.

Back in the UK by 1986, Graham was promoted to Sergeant and posted to RAF Cranwell. There his duties included assisting at the centre which provided medical cover for the Station's ab-Initio-Officers Flying Training Programme. In the course of his 16 months at Cranwell Graham Banks was often detached to other units and he also became qualified for field medical work. The end result of this extensive medical background was his posting in November 1987 to the Aeromedical Centre at Brize Norton as an instructor.

His duties at Brize continue to alternate between routine and emergency. On the routine side, up to ten students a month from the three Services come to learn about aeromedical work. The first two weeks are spent on the Ground Phase, which means classroom and equipment handling duties, while the second two weeks are devoted to the Flying Phase. Two or three students at a time go on flights to Germany, Cyprus,

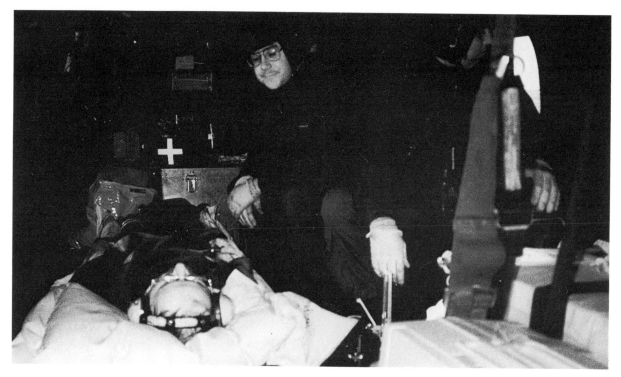

Ascension and the Falklands — actually doing the work for which they have been trained.

On the operational side Graham can and has been called to help on many diverse occasions. An Army lorry turns over on Cyprus crushing its occupants. A Navy ship puts into an American port for a sailor to have an appendix operation, then return to his UK home. During the build up to the Gulf War, there were accidents producing cases for treatment and return to the UK. When the war started there was concern, but this was followed by relief when only light Allied casualties materialized. Post-war there was the recovery of prisoners and the scaling down of aeromedical activities. 'We've had a hand too,' Flight Sergeant Graham Banks concluded, 'in the return of the British hostages from Beirut. Every case is different, but calls for the application of what we were taught, and we are now teaching others. It's a rewarding job.'

George Nute

It is said that NCOs run armies and NCO Engineers the air forces. This may be taking their contribution a shade too far, but there is no doubt as to the thoroughness of their early training and the length of varied engineering experience. The RAF is as full of them, as plums in a good pudding, so it is perhaps unfair to select one at RAF Brize Norton while all are making such worthwhile contributions. Nevertheless, Warrant Office George Nute typifies what it takes to keep aircraft flying. His contribution to the Royal Air Force was, at the time of writing this account, 37 years.

To begin at George's beginning, he is and looks a Cornishman. He was born and educated at Redruth. While Cornwall attracts holiday makers and tourists, there has never been a surplus of work there for the local inhabitants. Friends in his village shop suggested the RAF to George, and he joined at the age of 16 as an aircraft apprentice, signing on initially for 12 years. His first three years were spent at RAF Halton. George says the training there was thorough but hard and the regime in those days was tough.

Above George Nute in his office at the hub of Brize Norton's engineering activities around Base Hangar.

Above right Early RAF days. Aircraftman George Nute at the beginning of his Service career.

At the end of the three years, as a Junior technician, George Nute was posted to a Mosquito target towing flight at RAF Chivenor, North Devon. There were also Vampires and Hunters at the Station and for the next eight years he played his part in a typical Air Force setting. His first overseas detachment came in 1957 when he went to No.208 Squadron flying Hunters in Cyprus at the time of the EOKA trouble. George later moved to Jordan where he met King Hussein. In 1958 he returned to Chivenor and remained there for the next two years. In 1960 it was again off to the Middle East — to Aden this time with No.8 Squadron of Hunters. There were also short detachments to what was then Southern Rhodesia, Bahrain and Kuwait. George was promoted to Corporal during a tour at Aden (1961) and he was in Kuwait when that little country was earlier threatened by a big country called Iraq.

He returned to RAF St. Mawgan, on the north coast of Cornwall, in 1962 to work on Shackletons of No.42 Squadron. This involved him in many long (12-14 hour) flights. One flight of 19 hours took him to Canada. His time at St Mawgan included meeting an old Halton friend, being Best Man at the wedding and later marrying the Bridesmaid. George was 26 at the time and the couple began their married life in a caravan behind a pub before being able to rent a house. That was in 1963. At the end of 1964 George Nute, his wife and their eight-week-old son went out to RAF Seletar, Singapore, arriving on Christmas Eve to join 209 Squadron flying Single and Twin Pioneer aircraft. For the next three years George worked on these aircraft supporting Army operations with Gurkha troops in Malaysia, Borneo and Sarawak.

George Nute was promoted to Sergeant in 1965 and was posted to RAF Lyneham

George Nute *(centre background)* accompanies Mrs Thatcher on a visit to RAF Brize Norton.

in 1967 where he did First Line servicing on Britannias and Comet 4s until the former moved to Brize Norton in 1970. George stayed with Britannias until 1975, enjoying frequent trips to the United States and Canada, to Delhi and Katmandu — flying Gurkha troops from the last to their garrison in Hong Kong. His five years at Brize was followed by a brief spell on Wessex helicopters at Odiham. Then came promotion to Flight Sergeant and yet another posting, this time to the Nimrod Major Servicing Unit at Kinloss, Scotland, in charge of a major servicing team. During May 1980 the Nutes returned to St Mawgan where George served another three years on Nimrods. His travels were not yet over. After servicing Hawks at RAF Valley in Wales, he went to RAF Gibraltar to look after the visiting aircraft section. There George and his wife lived at beautiful Catalan Bay and visited all parts of Spain, Portugal and North Africa. They look back on that posting as a three year holiday.

On his promotion to warrant officer in 1987, which would mean yet another posting, George pestered the Personnel Management Centre at RAF Innsworth, Gloucester, for somewhere in south-west England. However, the personnel people are well known for their warped sense of humour and the Nutes were sent to eastern Scotland. George arrived at RAF Leuchars, Fifeshire, in March 1988 to work on Phantoms, and he remained there until his post was disestablished in March 1988. Brize Norton constitutes his last tour of duty before he leaves the Royal Air Force in February 1993. At Base Hangar, George Nute gives the same service and devotion to duty he has applied throughout his long career. In spite of the ups and downs during 37 years service, George says — if he could turn the clock back to age 16 — he would do it all again. He talks of missing the challenges and, more importantly, comradeship and loyalty — gifts hard to find in modern day civilian life. He will retire to his own house in Gloucestershire, but admits a secret longing finally to live in his native Cornwall.

Jim Wilcox

This book could not have been written without the help and support provided by Flight Lieutenant Jim Wilcox, Community Relations Officer at RAF Brize Norton. He made the arrangements, set up meetings, laid on photographs and checked countless drafts. All was done on top of his more than full-time job as CRO. Brize is a high profile Station and Jim's duties range from handling local issues to looking after the world's Press. Industry and commerce have teams of publicity people and agencies attempting to achieve the same results. They could learn a lot from Jim's pragmatic approach. The RAF has certainly got itself a bargain.

What does a Community Relations Officer do? Well, it would be easier to make a short list of what he does not do. In modern-day jargon, the CRO provides an interface between the Station and the outside world. An aviation-minded schoolboy wants information or a picture — his request is dealt with by the CRO. The Foreign Secretary is landing in a couple of hours time and the media wish to interview him — the CRO will see to it. A group of councillors are visiting the Station, an ATC party would like a flight, there is to be an Open Day, a Charity Night, a visiting celebrity or a noise problem — and it is over to the Community Relations Officer to organize, allocate, arrange and/or placate. His in-tray is always overflowing, his several telephones seldom stop ringing.

Physically Jim Wilcox is a solid-looking individual. One feels that bumping into him would be like trying to deflect a battletank. It comes as no surprise that he has been a keen sportsman and won his RAF athletics colours for tug-of-war at the age of 54. Incidentally, his son Robert, also in the Royal Air Force, was in the same team. Jim applies this no-nonsense solidity to his work and, to their surprise, the Press people interested in Britain's largest air base. 'All media activity concerning the

Jim Wilcox, in his official capacaity as Brize Norton's Community Relations Officer, with the media.

The man at the far end of the rope is Jim Wilcox, RAF (Retired), CRO at Brize Norton and a great grandfather.

Station,' he tells them, 'comes through me. That's the rule.'

The familiar stocky figure of Jim Wilcox has become something of a legend among the reporters, photographers and camera crews who attend Press briefings at Brize. They have come to know that he is in control and will not be shifted whatever the pressure. The Gulf War, for example, brought many pressures to bear — the troops going out, the casualties that might come back, the many varied and exciting demonstrations of Brize skills. It was all grist to the media mill, but Jim had seen it before. During 1961, when Iraq invaded Kuwait for the first time, he was on signal and cipher work. Jim knows his RAF and other Services, has witnessed and worked with the troubles caused by wars. 'Nowadays,' he says, 'wars are far quicker because they are more intense. It is a case of getting the intelligence and response build-up right before beginning to fight.'

Jim, an only child, stems from a tiny village on the Shropshire-Welsh border. He grew up during the Second World War well away from the disruptions caused by that conflict. An occasional aircraft — mostly friendly — flew over his rural location. Later, when Jim was 16, the quiet life moved him to try and see some of the world. His first choice was the Royal Navy, but it rejected him because of colour blindness. He then applied to join both the Army and the RAF. The Army seemed a bit too keen. 'Just pack your bag and get down to Chepstow,' they wrote. 'They appeared desperate for people,' Jim recalls, 'so I waited for the Royal Air Force to reply.' He accepted 'the King's shilling' during 1948 and joined the RAF as an administrative apprentice. This was not the sinecure it sounds. In those days the RAF was very much spit-and-polish, backed by strict discipline. For example, RAF apprentices were not allowed to be out after 10 p.m. There was a bed check and the apprentice not actually in bed or standing to attention by it was charged with being absent. Jim had his share of charges, which in turn meant more polishing, scrubbing, peeling potatoes and doubling round barrack squares wearing full webbing equipment and carrying a rifle at high port. However, despite everything, he passed out with flying colours in the top group of his class. Shortly afterwards he was made up to Corporal, then Sergeant and Flight Sergeant engaged on a wide range of administration duties.

Jim is an enthusiast about administration. 'That's what it is all about. Organizing, keeping everything moving yet under control!' The RAF training he received, Jim contends, was very thorough. 'We knew more about administration as airmen in those days than most of the more senior ranks today. Moreover, as administrative assistants, we were expected to cope in depth and unsupervised with any of the widely ranging administrative tasks that were part of everyday life in most RAF Stations.' He also satisfied his desire to travel— his many tours abroad including Holland, Germany, Egypt and Christmas Island. Jim believes that the part of his career which gave him the most satisfaction was when he became a warrant officer. 'It represented the top of my profession, the peak I had been working towards for many years.'

Obtaining a commission was another peak. Today Flight Lieutenant Jim Wilcox has left the active end and is serving as a Retired Officer. This means that, although continuing to wear uniform, he is exempt from parades and certain chores like Station Duty Officer. 'I don't get the pay either,' he adds wryly. Jim is married with three grown-up children, five grandchildren and one great granddaughter. He lives near Gloucester and each working day drives to and from RAF Brize Norton over the Cotswolds. His off-duty hours, when the media and others are not ringing him at home, are spent on many pastimes, hobbies and sports. He gardens, plays skittles in the local league and helps local organizations. He did not want anything written about him, but for once was overruled.

George Sizeland

Sports parachutists occupy a high position on the scale of human bravery. Military parachutists are higher still, and both agree that to have become an RAF parachute jumping instructor is to be at the pinnacle of that profession. Apart from the sustained courage needed to make a career out of jumping from aircraft, PJIs risk their lives again and again for their pupils, also while testing new equipment and techniques. No.1 Parachute Training School at RAF Brize Norton is a special place manned by special people. It was, therefore, particularly interesting how person after person said that the parachutist who should be written about was Squadron Leader George Sizeland MBE, Officer Commanding Training Co-ordination and Resources.

Physially and mentally George is a big man, big in stature and outlook. A keen rugby player in his youth, one can visualize those 6 ft and 15 stone charging through his opponents. Forty-five years and hundreds of parachute jumps later, George Sizeland is still larger than life, as well as contributing to the life of the School. One of his unofficial jobs has been to build up a unique collection of parachuting exhibits and memorabilia which it is hoped will be preserved by the RAF Museum or some similar Establishment devoted to the history of aviation.

To begin at the RAF beginning, George Sizeland lied about his birth date so that he could join as early as possible. In those early post-war days of 1946, the Services

George Sizeland MBE receives a presentation to record his 35 years as an RAF parachute jumping instructor with Airborne Forces.

Above George Sizeland showing Prince Philip pictures of parachute activities during a Royal Visit to Brize Norton.

were still somewhat dislocated. The Air Force in fact recruited George as a parachute jumping instructor, and he was somewhat surprised that this first required him to attend a physical training instructor's course at Cosford. He was more surprised on being posted to Gosport in error. After arriving at Cosford and receiving a rollocking for being late, George was informed that the eight-week PTI Course was extended to 18 weeks. This was so he and others could appear as an RAF gymnastic team at the Royal Tournament followed by a recruiting tour of England and Wales.

After qualifying as a physical training instructor, his role in show business and his promotion to Corporal, George was posted to RAF Brize Norton before the US Air Force arrived. He says (to his recollection) there was no town of Carterton, no housing estates, no married quarters off base and no one seemed to own a car. Accommodation for airmen was the standard wooden huts each containing 20 beds and a central stove. The boiler in the gym, which still stands opposite Admin HQ, was lit each morning for showers so George moved in and remained there, undiscovered, during his first Brize tour.

In 1949 he went to No.1 Parachute Training School, then at RAF Upper Heyford. The basic training was the same as now, but much else was primitive. Instead of specialized clothing, parachutists wore the everyday hairy blue battledress, a rubber jumping hat and leather soled boots with much metal on the soles and heels. The latter produced what felt like an electric shock when hitting the ground. There was a 28 ft diameter parachute, but no reserve, so that malfunctions resulted in serious injuries or worse. At least the old Dakotas were reliable and gave a modest dropping speed of only 90 knots.

For two years as a Sergeant instructor, George taught the parachuting units of the Territorial Army. The TAs did their training in the evenings and weekends. Thus the work was interesting though demanding due to the unsociable hours. Suddenly George was switched to 'the real thing', helping the SAS to combat terrorists deep in the Malaysian jungle. Formerly patrols had spent six weeks moving into the area and

Above left George Sizeland with a paratrooper model in the museum he created.

six weeks moving out again. It was decided to drop patrols in the densest jungle to combat the terrorists directly. Helicopters could not be used so parachuting was the only option. As the trees were 200 ft tall, the intention was for the parachute to catch on the top branches after which the parachutist would lower himself with a 240 ft line. George volunteered for this after two men had lost their lives during preliminary tests.

He became proficient at abseiling inside a hangar at Singapore, then came the day of his first trial descent into the jungle. There, his own weight, combined with that of heavy equipment, took him through the treetops and straight down to the jungle floor. After regaining consciousness several hours later, George found both his legs were badly damaged. Terrified of being in the jungle after dark, he kept crawling downhill and eventually reached some paddy fields where two Gurkhas found him. A long stay in hospital followed.

Later, after testing military parachuting in the thin air over 4,000 ft high Rhodesia, George spent two years at RAF Abingdon learning about free falling. By then the types of aircraft out of which he jumped had been increased from Dakotas and Hastings to Andovers, Argosies, Beverleys and the near perfect Hercules. In 1967 George Sizeland was commissioned, after which he returned to No.1 Parachute Training School. A period as Flight Commander and Operations Officer was followed by promotion to Flight Lieutenant. George became responsible for the training of all potential instructors, both in the UK and from overseas. Forty-three Foreign and Commonwealth countries have received basic parachute training at No.1 PTS of which 18 different nationalities have progressed to instructional standard.

In the Spring of 1971 came George Sizeland's supreme test — to train the heir to the Throne. At the time Prince Charles, who was learning to fly at RAF Cranwell, wanted to make a parachute descent. George admits to extreme nervousness with that assignment though, as history records, he did not lose a future King. On the day, he briefed Prince Charles before going aboard the command boat in Studland Bay. There he made the drop calculations and passed them to the aircraft. Prince Charles then did everything well and went on to face the world's Press.

For George there followed a two-year detachment with the Army at Aldershot which was soon followed by the School's move from Abingdon to Brize Norton. It was 27 years since he had last seen Brize as a Corporal PTI. Among other tasks at Brize Norton, No.1 PTS was training both Regular and Territorial Army soldiers, also personnel from all three Services on Adventurous Parachute Training. As for George, he spent two years as a Junior Staff Officer in London and moved on to RAF Gutersloh as a physical education officer. During a major exercise there he was awarded the MBE for his services to Airborne Forces. He returned to the UK as a Squadron Leader, first to command the Physical Education Squadron at RAF Halton, then for his last tour at No.1 PTS Brize Norton at the age of 52. This he celebrated by running a 26-mile marathon. With six months to go to his 55th birthday George requested a Retired Officer post — to impart his wealth of parachuting knowledge to those following him — and this was granted. Married to a WAAF Telephonist in 1950, George and Iris have two sons (RAF and Royal Marines) and three daughters.

Keith Filbey

During the months of visiting and learning about RAF Brize Norton for this book, certain questions kept coming to mind. How could one person carry sole responsibility for such a large and complex place? What sort of upbringing and training was needed to become a Station Commander? Did he sleep at nights? Throughout the time of book research, Group Captain Keith Filbey could be seen around the base — with the flying Squadrons and in the engineering workshops, meeting the highest in the land one moment and chatting to a local farmer the next.

Keith Filbey, Station Commander at RAF Brize Norton.

An interview with him, only undertaken after the whole book had been written, answered many questions. In fact it put the last pieces about RAF Brize Norton in place.

Keith Filbey stems from Essex. His father was in the RAF, retiring as a Squadron Leader to take up teaching and become a headmaster. At the same time his mother took up nursing. Thus in both cases there was a serving/caring family background. No pressure was put on the son to join anything. A film about a flight across Africa prompted him towards a flying career. After weighing up civil and military training, he opted for the latter. There was a secondary consideration, his keenness on sport which the Service provided in plenty. So he applied to the RAF and went to Cranwell as a cadet in October 1966.

After graduating and completing his advanced flying training, Keith Filbey joined No.214 Squadron at RAF Marham, near King's Lynn. There he flew Victor tankers, thus commencing a career-long interest in air-to-air refuelling. Keith Filbey completed tours as a co-pilot and as a captain before becoming an AAR instructor. He was promoted to Squadron Leader in July 1976 — less than ten years after joining the RAF — and became a Flight Commander on No.51 Squadron at RAF Wyton, near Huntingdon, flying Nimrods.

Below right When Keith Filbey took over command of Brize Norton, the Station was more like a building site — which explains this picture.

There is a great deal more to the RAF than flying aircraft, and for five years from April 1978 Keith Filbey flew desks. He did personnel work at an MOD Establishment near Gloucester. This was followed by the Advanced Staff Course at RAF Staff College, Bracknell. He was then posted to HQ No.1 Group at RAF Bawtry, Yorkshire, as a staff officer with responsibility for tanker operations. Later, in 1983, he moved to MOD, Whitehall, where once again his responsibilities included operational policy for all tanker aircraft. His career pattern was now clearly established.

In July 1983, Keith Filbey was promoted to Wing Commander and came to RAF Brize Norton where he commanded No.216 Squadron flying TriStars in their twin air transport and air-to-air refuelling roles. On completion of his command tour in December 1986 he was posted back to the MOD in London where he became responsible for the operational policy of the RAF's entire air-to-air refuelling activities. Further moves to HQ No.1 Group at RAF Upavon and Strike Command at RAF High Wycombe, now as a Group Captain, followed until June 1990. Then, after completing a VC10 C MK1 course at No.241 OCU, enabling him to fly these aircraft from RAF Brize Norton, he became Station Commander in mid-December 1990 — on the eve of the Gulf War.

The RAF does not pause to take breath when commanders change over. The situation immediately greeting Group Captain Filbey was of an entire Squadron (101 flying VC10 tankers) being detached to the Gulf, together with the Tactical Communications Wing, as described elsewhere in this book. Air Transport operations at Brize had multiplied to fourteen times the peace-time rate. Confronted with such a situation, Keith Filbey recalls his two main concerns. The first was the fear of losing some of his people which at the time seemed a strong possibility. The second was that the Station, now his responsibility, must continue to play its part as an essential contributor to the Allied effort in the Gulf, preferably without making an avoidable error. As it turned out, he was amazed by the enthusiasm and energies of everyone around him. If anything, he found himself having to rein people back rather than exhorting them to greater effort, while keeping the powers-that-be off their backs. There was little paperwork at the time, though he ruefully observed that he had made up for it since.

Below Two veteran Brize Norton captains — Bob Henderson and Keith Filbey.

What of lessons learned during his formative years in the RAF, also from his dedication to air refuelling? Keith Filbey gives priority to true teamwork. If a team is

working well, whatever the task, it can achieve impressive results. As to the importance of air refuelling, he points out that the two most recent wars in which the RAF was involved — Falklands and Gulf — necessitated AAR both to get there and to fight.

He has his own memorable experiences of air refuelling. The one that gives him most satisfaction took place in the mid-eighties. From 1983 to 1986 Keith Filbey was responsible for re-forming No.216 Squadron and ensuring that his crews set high standards of air transportation and air-to-air refuelling. The culmination of this was when he led his aircrft and three waves of Tornados to reinforce Masirah, South Oman as part of Exercise Swift Sword. The TriStar tankers, each with two Tornados and a VC10 tanker of No.101 Squadron in close formation, flew non-stop to Oman. There, as it happened, the House of Commons Defence Committee was waiting. As it also happened, the TriStars and Tornados were due to arrive at 13.30 local time. They did so — on the dot.

What strengths does Keith Filbey think tanker crews need? He believes the task requires a combination of patience, flexibility and a 'can-do' spirit. He argues that, while flying a relatively slow and unwieldy fuel tanker aircraft, its pilot also has to think in terms of thirsty fast-jets. It requires a sort of dual mental process applied to and governing basic piloting skills. It requires practice and takes time to learn, and tanker crews are always learning.

What kind of leadership can be expected from an Air Transport/Air-to-Air Refuelling pilot? How does someone of that ilk, promoted to command the largest Station in the RAF, judge people? Again Keith Filbey contends he is always learning though he has gained and applied some very helpful clues. He likes people to be positive and sure of their ground, to radiate and, demonstrate genuine efficiency. He does not like vacillation or bluff. He also admits to not always accepting the first proposal of the first person selling an idea to him. He likes to bounce such ideas off others before making the decision and, of course, taking the responsibility.

How does he relax in what can be a 25 hour day job? 'Well I love the job, RAF Brize Norton is an exciting Station with nearly 4400 personnel. There is a lot going on and I enjoy the buzz that this generates. Everything that happens inside the wire (and a lot that happens outside) is my responsibility and I find it an exciting challenge. It is very rewarding to see the team effort produce the right results. It is also a privilege to be running a place like Brize Norton and I aim to enjoy every minute. I especially value the opportunity to meet such a wide cross-section of people from Cabinet ministers to county cricketers, from the Town Mayor to the Vice Chancellor of Oxford University. It is a one-off tour that will never be repeated.'

To these activities, Group Captain Keith Filbey adds sports which, apart from aviation, attracted him to the RAF in the first place. His present short list of sports includes squash, tennis, golf and skiing. He also enjoys flying, classical music, jazz, reading and meeting people. Last but not least, there is his personal priority — family life with his wife Anne, son and daughter. Summing up the subject of this brief profile, Keith Filbey succeeds in applying simplicity to complexity, and that is one of the most difficult feats to achieve in present day life.

Chapter 12

AIR-TO-AIR REFUELLING

One of the most interesting activities at RAF Brize Norton is that of air-to-air refuelling. It is both preached and practised at the Station, which houses the RAF's AAR School teaching AAR techniques and No.101 Squadron whose VC10 tanker aircraft are engaged on AAR duties.

The School is another of Brize Norton's lodger Units which, like the rest, plays a full part in the life of the Station. For administration purposes, it is attached to No.241 Operational Conversion Unit and is in the same building as the flight simulators. All pilots of RAF tankers and receiver aircraft go through the School, as do many Commonwealth and other approved air crews. Nationals attending courses have included French and Italians, Canadians and Australians, Saudis and Omanis. School instructors also gave AAR tuition to US Navy and Marines personnel during the Gulf War.

Regarding RAF pilots, these receive tuition on five aircraft AAR systems — VC10, Tristar, Victor, Hercules and Buccaneer. The last incidentally is the only RAF fighter to have both tanker and receiver capability. With the Buccaneer, wing drop tanks are used to carry the extra fuel by which one fighter plane can refuel another. It is called the 'buddy system', and a Buccaneer can be converted to a tanker role in half an hour. The buddy system, which is one of many AAR techniques, notably extends combat air patrols, and up to ten hours have been logged. Today there are fleets of airborne tankers routinely engaged on air-to-air refuelling operations. As with the buddy system, applications have been so developed and refined that ultimately crew fatigue rather than fuel burn determines the duration of sorties.

But to begin at the beginning. It is some 70 years since fuel was transferred by pipeline between two aircraft in flight. There are two main methods of doing so. The first is by a telescopic boom fitted under the rear fuselage of the tanker. The boom is lowered and extended to engage with the receiver. It can also be 'flown' into position by fitting aerofoils. The boom system was developed at Boeing and is used by the US Air Force. The second is the British probe and drogue system pioneered by Flight Refuelling, and the US Navy, RAF and other air forces employ this method.

The probe part is defined as 'a forward projecting tube fitted with a special nozzle and mounted in such a position that it is clearly visible to the pilot of the receiver aircraft.' The drogue assembly — or 'basket' as it is commonly called — is attached to the rear end of a flexible hose from the tanker. When the hose is trailed, the drogue, which has a conical para-type device, acts as a stabilizer as well as an aiming point for the receiver probe. There are many refinements to the probe and drogue method to be described later. To give some examples here, the pilot of the receiver aircraft directing the probe is helped by a system of lights on the tanker. At night there are special reflectors on the drogue itself to assist him. As for the tanker crew, the air engineer on

the flight deck can view the hose and drogue, also the probe link-up, by means of a rearward viewing television camera.

The tail end of a VC10 with refuelling hose extended.

Hoses from the tanker aircraft are wound on to and trailed from drum units. Each VC10 tanker has a single hose drum unit (HDU MK 17B), housed under the rear fuselage, and a pair of MK32 wing pods. These VC10 tankers contain five extra fuel cells installed in what was the passenger cabin. The K2 version carries an offload capability of 165,000 lb, and the K3 carries 175,000 lb. Some of Brize Norton's TriStars have extra tanks fitted so they can undertake AAR roles if required. These TriStar tankers have nine extra cells under the cabin floor to hold an additional 100,000 lb of fuel and incorporate a double hose drum unit under the rear fuselage. However, VC10 tankers represent the RAF's main AAR fleet while the TriStars are used more for their considerable passenger and freight carrying capabilities.

The hoses which run between the drum units and the drogues are constructed somewhat like a motor car tyre. They have outer and inner skins of thick rubber sandwiching steel ply and a helix of steel wire. These metal reinforcements run the entire length of the hose from drum to drogue. Regarding the two types of AAR units used by the RAF, their leading particulars are as follows:

Leading Particulars	Hose Drum Unit MK17B	Wing Pod Unit MK32
Hose Length	81ft	48ft
Hose Diameter	3 in	2 in
Delivery Pressure	50lb/in^2	50lb/in^2
Refuel Rate	4000lb/min	3000lb/min

No.101 Squadron personnel inspect the centre housing of a refuelling hose unit. Other tankers of the Squadron are in the background.

It takes a fighter aircraft about five minutes to receive 10,000 lb (5 tonnes) of fuel, whereas a large transport would require up to half an hour for the transfer of 40-60,000 lb (25-30 tonnes). Air-to-air refuelling was routinely used when flying combat aircraft to the Gulf. These receivers, accompanied by tanker aircraft, completed the flight in nine hours. Combat planes and tankers travelled together at speeds of 550 miles per hour with each of the former being refuelled five or six times during the journey. Brize VC10 tankers regularly accompany fast jets across the Atlantic. They usually land at Goose Bay, Newfoundland, then proceed to air exercises over the Nevada Desert.

A VC10 tanker trailing central and wing hoses.

A VC10 tanker refuelling a VC10 passenger transport.

There is another important aspect of tanker aircraft such as the VC10 and TriStar. Using their usual and additional fuel, these versions can themselves cover great distances without landing. A VC10 tanker can take off from Brize Norton and fly direct to San Francisco, while a TriStar takes 13½ hours to reach Fiji — which is about as far as it can get round the globe before returning.

Although the probe and drogue, hose and drum concepts are simple in theory, their practical usage demands detailed design, precision engineering, thorough training for the participants and considerable practice. Bringing aircraft so close together during flight, then exchanging tons of fuel is both an exciting and exacting operation. Like most other successes by the RAF, a start is made in the classroom. The AAR School at Brize Norton contains cutaway examples of the main units utilized for flight refuelling, and even the beginner soon sees that there is more to the art than meets the eye. As if to emphasize this point, the School has a photographic display in one corner of what can go wrong — broken probes and wrecked drogues, hoses wrapped round receiver aircraft.

On the positive side, the AAR School has a hand-operated probe and drogue working exhibit which clearly demonstrates what is involved. The cutaway sections reveal how the nozzle profile of the probe matches the internal contours of the drogue's reception coupling. It also reveals that the probe, though appearing to be a simple tube, incorporates outer and inner concentric spring-loaded sleeves. As the probe nozzle enters the reception coupling, latching levers release an outer sleeve member of the probe. When the nozzle meets a seal ring in the reception coupling, both outer and inner probe sleeves are forced back against their springs. Simultaneously, the domed nose of the probe pushes open a cut-off valve in the reception coupling.

As both sides of the connection open, toggle-arm rollers engage an external annular groove in the probe nozzle. This locks all components in place, and they are correctly aligned for fuel transfer. The probe unit contains an emergency check valve

A TriStar tanker with refuelling hose trailed.

and 'weak link' section. In the event of excess loads during refuelling, the latter will fracture allowing disengagement. At the same time the emergency check valve will prevent loss of fuel from the tanker aircraft. These, therefore, are the main features of the probe and drogue mechanism. A little more, however, should be said about the drogue.

The drogue looks like and, as previously mentioned, is often called a basket. To take this comparison further, its construction is that of a light metal framework, the assembly resembling a basket with a ring of cloth round the rim. When the drogue is pulled up and into the tunnel by its winch, the unit collapses for stowage. When the drogue is trailed by the hose into the airstream, the cloth canopy expands the basket work to its maximum diameter. This expansion will allow the probe to enter the drogue reception coupling guided by the basket-like frame. When the hose is extended, its drogue produces a pull of approximately one ton because of the airspeed. To prevent this pull being conveyed to the receiver aircraft, the hose drum unit on the tanker partly winds in the hose, thus countering the pull. Another drogue feature is the rearward-facing ring of what look like reflectors on the cloth canopy. These

A Tornado receiving fuel from a TriStar.

'reflectors', used to guide receiver aircraft pilots at night, are gaseous tritium light sources known as Beta lights.

Moving back from the drogue and up the hose to its drum unit, the HDU MK17B is secured to the roof of an enclosed bay under the VC10 rear fuselage. Standing on the ground and looking up at the protrusion, one sees the hose tunnel with the drogue collapsed within it and an underside intake door. Visible also are three pairs of refuelling signal lights — red, orange and green. Each pair has a repeater light included in the air engineer's control panel on the flight deck.

The underside intake door is hinged at its forward end and opens inwards to admit ram air to deploy the drogue from the rear end of the tunnel. Door actuation is by a hydraulic jack controlled via a switch also on the air engineer's panel. To put it simply, if the door does not open, the hose cannot be trailed. After the hose has been trailed, a turbine pump within the HDU boosts the pressure of fuel supplied from the tanker to the required 50 lb/in2. On the VC10 tanker, this small turbine is driven by air from the anti-icing system. An electric motor in the HDU operates to limit the speed of the trail and to eliminate hose whip when the receiver aircraft makes

Above Another TriStar air-to-air refuelling operation; this time with a Phantom fighter.

Above left A pilot's view of a TriStar tanker.

Below A TriStar tanker tops up a VC10 tanker watched over by a Tornado.

A TriStar refuels a TriStar.

contact. It also drives the drum to wind in the hose. When the hose is fully wound on the drum, the latter is held by a ratchet brake. The HDU system on the TriStar has two such units (MK 17Ts) mounted side by side in a pressure box built within the cargo compartment.

Provision is made for trailing and releasing the hose in an emergency. The inner end of the hose is connected to a fuel feed pipe assembly by means of a spring-loaded ball lock. The spring can be released by energizing a solenoid at the fully trailed position.

The VC10 underwing mounted refuelling pod (MK32) is a streamlined self-contained unit which, like the fuselage fitted version, delivers fuel from the tanker to the receiver aircraft. As indicated in the leading particulars of the two units, the wing pod drum has a smaller diameter (2 in) and a shorter (48 ft) hose. A ram air turbine at

A flight refuelling hose drum unit Mk 17T as fitted to RAF and other tanker aircraft. *(Courtesy of Flight Refuelling)*

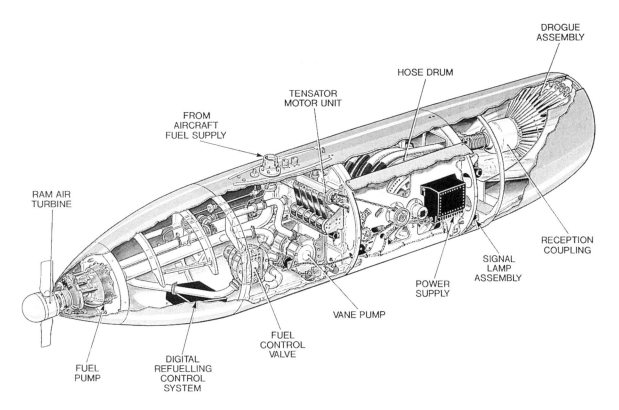

the nose of the pod drives a pump for trailing, transferring and winding-in operations. As with the main HDV, the wing pod units are controlled by the air engineer. The system utilizes digital electronic logic to operate and monitor the various mechanical and electro-hydraulic functions. These include hose trailing, fuel transferring and hose rewinding as just mentioned; also fuel flow and pressure, venting and emergency hose jettisoning. The electronic system enables rapid health assessment of the unit.

A cutaway drawing of a flight refuelling pod unit Mk 32B *(Courtesy of Flight Refuelling)*

Moving back again from the hose drum units into the tanker aircraft, the VC10 K2s and K3s at RAF Brize Norton have virtually been converted into flying bowsers. In addition to its own many fuel tanks — three in each side of the mainplane, one in the K3 tail fin and a large centre section tank in the lower fuselage — there are the added five cells in what used to be the passenger cabin. The whole aircraft envelope is threaded with fuel lines. These include feeds to the main engines; probe intake lines; transfer, vent and dump lines. All are under the control of the air engineer who also oversees air-to-air refuelling operations.

Two AAR aids notably help the air engineer of the tanker and the pilot in the receiver aircraft. The television camera, mounted amidships under the tanker fuselage, can be turned to view each of the three transfer areas — i.e. the trailing central or wing hose/drogues. This is shown on a screen immediately in front of the engineer and enables him to control the sequence of AAR operations. The other AAR aid is that of the coloured light system on the tanker hydraulic drum unit. These notably assist in allowing the refuelling operations to take place without breaking radio silence. As previously mentioned, they consist of red, amber and green lights. When the red light is on, this tells the pilot of the receiver aircraft not to engage the tanker drogue which may not, for example, be fully trailed. The amber light shows him that the hose has now been fully trailed and may be engaged. The green light indicates positive engagement and transference of fuel. When the pilot of the receiver aircraft wishes to disengage the probe from the drogue, he reduces speed

Right A TriStar refuelling a Tornado F3 over the Gulf.

Below right The television screen at an air engineer's work station, showing an aircraft approaching to be refuelled.

Below Thirsty Jaguars being refuelled by a VC10 over the Gulf.

to the point when a pre-determined pull-off point is reached, causing the probe and drogue to separate.

So much for the theory. What is air-to-air refuelling, as carried out by the RAF, like in practice? The best source of information — and demonstration — of this is to fly with a VC10 tanker of No.101 Squadron as its crews are constantly engaged on such operations. Flights range from regular training exercises to a war situation, such as the Gulf campaign. The Squadron's part in Operations Granby and Desert Storm has been related earlier in this book and the following account is that of a typical tanking exercise. It is also a typical receiving exercise for Squadrons of combat aircraft based round the British Isles. For air-to-air refuelling is not only a technique which requires thorough technical training by all concerned, but demands regular practice to make perfect.

At RAF Brize Norton, No.101 Squadron seem to keep to themselves across on the southern side of the airfield. The lucky person going flying with them first sees their headquarters building, servicing sheds and tanker aircraft far away and low on the landscape. On drawing nearer, the VC10 K2 and K3 tankers begin to make their presence felt. They are painted in a low visibility scheme of hemp colour with light grey undersides. They look very workaday when compared with the smartly finished passenger VC10s of No.10 Squadron.

A close-up of a flight refuelling drogue, showing it fully expanded. *(Courtesy of Flight Refuelling)*

Other external features of the tanker versions, apart from their hose units and television camera, are extra lights for night operations, also high visibility markings under the wings and fuselage — all acting as guides for correct positioning during the link-up operation.

Entry to the VC10 tanker aircraft is via a mobile steps unit to the front starboard side crew door. Another step inside reveals an interesting and practical layout. Immediately behind the flight deck — housing the captain, co-pilot, navigator and air engineer — there is a spacious and comfortable cabin, the width of the aircraft fuselage, which could be called a flying crew room. This cabin contains airline-style seats, kitchen and toilet facilities. The configuration is a very useful one because tanker crews have to undergo long hours travelling, trailing, circling while waiting and returning to base. The arrangement also means that the tanker aircraft can, and more often than not does, carry its own ground crew. This makes the aircraft an independent operating Unit when deploying to a base other than its home one. No.101 Squadron is often faced with, and seems to thrive on, such deployments. Its personnel have acquired entrepreneurial outlooks, making the best of every move whatever the circumstances.

After the newcomer has become acquainted with flight deck and crew cabin layouts — also personal belongings, tool kits and other gear brought along for that

A tanker view of a Harrier being refuelled, and two more standing by. *(Courtesy of Flight Refuelling)*

exercise — a visit is made into the rear fuselage fuel compartment. Access is through a door in the rear bulkhead of the crew cabin. At this advanced stage, the engineers and Loadmaster are making their pre-flight checks as are the two pilots who, with the navigator, have spent the last two to three hours planning the forthcoming operation. Not only do their plans have to cover every aspect of the flight, they must also include the link-ups with receiver aircraft which will take place during it. Air-to-air refuelling can be likened to a game of three dimensional chess.

Gradually, as the time of departure approaches, everyone begins to settle down. There is an underlying discipline in the way each individual acts within the overall situation. The flight deck personnel go through a well-rehearsed sequence of checks and procedures. The ground crew personnel find seats, strap themselves in and exchange remarks with the cabin supervisor who has eyes for the finest details. A loose item, an unclipped strap — he immediately has it put right. Meanwhile, the four Conway engines of the VC10 are running, at what seems a great distance, down aft. One feels the power more than hears the noise.

Following take-off, the VC10 tanker is set on a noise abatement climb of 290 knots and 3000 ft/min. The course is also set — up the Pennine backbone of England, over the Lowlands and Highlands of Scotland to an offshore air refuelling area (ARA), of which there are several round the British Isles. For this exercise the tanker will move from one area to another to meet various types of receiver aircraft sent up by different Squadrons.

To a mere onlooker, these air-to-air refuelling operations could seem uncanny. One moment the tanker aircraft is flying in what appears to be empty sky. The next moment two combat aircraft materialize off the wing tip. At what looks like a nod from the tanker captain, the receiver planes slide backwards to begin the link-up sequence. The options afforded by the VC10 tanker — central, one wing pod or both pod hoses — are all used on such exercises for the receiver pilots to gain experience. Pilots of combat aircraft like the VC10 as a tanker because the hoses remain stable when trailed, and the fast delivery rate means less plugged-in time.

These first two receiver aircraft wish to take fuel from the central hose drum unit in turn. They are now invisible to the tanker crew apart from the picture seen by the air engineer in his television screen. The first fast jet noses in, engages perfectly and takes on fuel. The second has two . . . three attempts before lining up. At moments such as these — when speeds, heights and air conditions have to be taken into account — it becomes obvious that the technique is neither simple nor automatic.

A receiver view of a VC10 tanker refuelling two Harriers via wing pod units. (Courtesy of Flight Refuelling)

After both are refuelled, the first pair of combat aircraft show themselves to starboard before sliding sideways and downwards out of sight. Almost immediately, two more of the same aircraft appear — again seemingly from nowhere. This time the pair wish to refuel from the wing pods. The air engineer remains at his television-equipped control panel, but others may watch the link-up through side windows in the tank compartment. With both the wing hoses trailing and the second pair plugged into them, the relative motions of the three aircraft become apparent. The impression is that the three are floating, which they are, on thin air — kept up there by their speeds and aerofoils. One can almost, but not quite, see the air flowing over the wing surfaces.

After three pairs of fast jets have refuelled and slid away the tanker banks and heads for another air refuelling area. If the tanker aircraft has to wait for the customers to turn up, it 'racetracks' — i.e. circles. A typical AAR training session will take about four hours during which some 10-12 aircraft are refuelled. Different speeds, heights and weather conditions add to testing variants experienced by the receiver aircraft. Other tests include refuelling while maintaining strict radio silence and link-ups at night. Afterwards the performances of all concerned are discussed and recorded. These exercises are maintained to ensure the high level of efficiency expected from the Royal Air Force.

No one knows when, but every Service man and woman is aware that training exercises can change in an instant to actual operations. Apart from their invaluable training role the VC10 tankers of No.101 Squadron are ready to participate in all situations, such as air defence, ground attack, airborne early warning, fleet air support and maritime patrol. In operations where several types of aircraft are used the tanker often has the best radio equipment and, if directed to do so, assumes control of that group for that mission.

The use of air-to-air refuelling now plays an important part in RAF tactical planning. Without AAR support, combat aircraft take off for a mission loaded with weapons and sufficient fuel to cover the entire operation. With AAR, the combat aircraft can take off with more weapons and less fuel because they can top up either before, during or after the mission. Taken to its logical conclusion, this means that the maximum of weapons can be delivered by the minimum of aircraft. Possible risks to valuable aircraft and invaluable pilots are noticeably lessened by applying the AAR factor.

A notable example of this, which won worldwide admiration at the time, was the

A Brize Norton TriStar tanker refuelling Tornados.

'Black Buck' raid carried out by the RAF during an early part of the Falklands Campaign. Two Vulcan bombers — one the prime aircraft and the other a stand-by airborne reserve — took off from Ascension Island. They were accompanied by no fewer than 11 Victor tankers. As the formation flew south, Victors topped up other Victors so that, at any given point, all aircraft had sufficient fuel to reach either Ascension or a diversion airfield. By the use of these AAR procedures, the Vulcan delivered 21 x 1000 lb bombs.

This example shows how the use of air-to-air refuelling allows aircraft to operate over an extended combat radius restricted only by another factor — that of crew fatigue. Even the latter may be alleviated in several ways, one of which is by medication. During the Falklands campaign again, carried out as it was over the great distances of the South Atlantic, RAF aircrews made use of medication with no side-effects. The Service's aeromedical expertise and experience ensured both proper treatment and careful monitoring.

For combat air patrols (CAPS), loiter time is a major consideration. It has been established that air-to-air refuelling triples the time on station without increasing crew fatigue. This is now a standard feature for air defence pilots enabling more efficient use of resources. Not only is the payload/range/endurance equation improved, it also allows rapid introduction of combat aircraft to a theatre of operations. In the cases of transport flights, maritime patrols and use of aircraft in early warning roles, AAR provides the continuous surveillance support required. Here, crew fatigue can be overcome by carrying a second team thereby allowing the first a rest period aboard the aircraft. With a succession of tankers acting as back-up, the key aircraft can remain aloft for days and nights at a time.

The rapidly changing geopolitical situation and the lessons learned from recent conflicts have shown the need for a new kind of aerial warfare called combined air operations. By this is meant the use of air power in composite force packages comprising combinations of fighters and bombers, reconnaissance and surveillance aircraft operating together. This approach exploits the capabilities that bring each together. The 'adhesive' for such a force would be the tanker aircraft maintaining filling stations, as it were, in the sky.

Tactical air wings intended to fight as a combined unit are already taking shape. They are being designed to support out-of-area missions such as that which arose in the Gulf and could occur again anywhere in the world. Aviation advances, particularly those involving air-to-air refuelling, have shrunk the world sufficiently for such counter measures to be effective. The tactical wings can be structured in many shapes and sizes as required for their designated roles. One combination would work with ground forces, another provide rapid deployment to a trouble area. Once committed, the wing could perform both defensive and offensive operations. Flexibility and interchangeability would be mandatory among aircraft and crews, with the air-to-air refuelling core element making the rest effective.

Air-to-air refuelling and the uses to which it can be put are the final pieces of the jigsaw picture making up RAF Brize Norton. The Station can now be viewed as a whole and, once the parts are together, what an amazingly diverse picture is presented — gateway for Service passengers; home to several very different and active Squadrons; Schools for pilots, parachutists, air movements and medical specialists; a workshop for aeroengineers, a base for many other experts. How best to sum up such a place that for over half a century has seen a World War and a Cold War, helped in so many subsequent emergencies and campaigns? The Station motto, though applying to transients, applies just as well to its residents: 'Transire Confidenter' — Pass Through Confidently.

Appendix

VINTAGE YEAR

The year 1991 proved to be a vintage one for RAF Brize Norton. It began with a war and ended with a visit by HM the Queen. Much else happened in between, so the best way is to tell it month by month.

January

Between 5 and 9 January No.10 Squadron flew the Prime Minister, John Major, to the Gulf where he visited the British Forces and liaised with allied forces and Arab heads of State. During January also, the Foreign Secretary and the Secretary of State for Defence flew similar routes with 10 Squadron. This Brize Norton Squadron discontinued scheduled flights on 16 January — the day the Gulf War started — which released its VC10s to play a full part in the deployment and resupply of troops in the Middle East.

With regard to No.101 Squadron flying VC10 K tankers, virtually the whole Squadron was detached to Riyadh. On the last day of January, 101 Squadron proudly announced their 101st sortie for Operation Desert Storm with zero sorties lost.

As for No.216 Squadron's war efforts, these were continuous, with each TriStar type performing in its optimum mode. The TriStar C2s carried maximum passenger loads, the KC1s invariably handled 40 tonnes of freight, and the K1s tanked either between the UK and the Gulf or in the theatre of war. Two K1s were painted pale pink for desert camouflage and were inevitably nicknamed Pinky and Perky.

As the enormity of the task became apparent, RAF Brize Norton was reinforced to cope. No.4624 Auxiliary Air Force Movements Squadron was called up to assist, and two huge temporary hangars were erected to house the massive influx of freight. The Station had to deal with many extra aircraft including Skyair and Anglo Cargo 707s, Kuwaiti Airlines and Evergreen 747s, Air Europe 757s, Britannia 767s and Sabena DC10s.

Additionally, work to install Brize Norton's new refuelling system denied the use of three much needed aircraft parking bays. Moreover, as if to push the Station to its limits, Operation Blacktop was in force for lengthy periods to keep the runway, taxiways and roads clear of snow and ice, thus ensuring continuity of flights.

February

Although the inclement weather continued into February and made operations difficult, it only momentarily hindered reinforcement and resupply of Gulf forces — such was the drive to keep things moving. Besides moving a colossal amount of freight, VIPs came and went. After the Gulf War ended on 28 February, and with the freedom of Kuwait, a most memorable flight was the return of the British Ambassador to his Embassy. Despite being the shortest month, February 1991 was the busiest of that Brize Norton year. By the last day, the Station had broken all its previous records for monthly freight movement.

March

The Prime Minister flew by No.10 Squadron VC10 to Moscow on 4 March and continued to the Gulf to congratulate the British Forces on their successful operation. On 8 March the first of the two ceremonies to receive back the bodies of Servicemen killed in the war was held at RAF Brize Norton. HRH The Duke of Kent attended the ceremony, representing the Queen. On 19 March the second aircraft carrying bodies arrived at Brize Norton when again the Duke of Kent paid respects.

No.101 Squadron returned en masse on 13 March, all nine VC10 tanker aircraft arriving home between 14.00 and 16.00 hours. The crews received a rapturous welcome from their families, the Station, also both the outgoing and incoming Air Officers Commanding No.1 Group. No.10 Squadron was busy again with VVIP work on 15 March flying the Prime Minister to Bermuda.

April

No.10 Squadron resumed the Washington Dulles Schedules on 8 April as if all problems in Iraq had been dealt with, but on 9 April Operation Haven — the provision of safe haven for the Kurds — was launched. The first two flights were mounted by No.216 Squadron and, by the end of April, No.10 Squadron had completed 30 mercy missions to eastern Turkey.

In addition, No.10 Squadron handled the VVIP trips during April — another trip to Bermuda on the 11th, a trip to Istanbul on the 24th and one to Dublin on the 27th. In April also, Air Chief Marshal Sir Patrick Hine, Air Officer Commanding-in-Chief Strike Command, paid his farewell visit to RAF Brize Norton. As well as AOC-in-C, he had been the Joint Force Commander for all British Forces involved in the Gulf Campaign.

May

On Thursday 3 May No.216 Squadron resumed its Cyprus schedule, and on Friday 4 May the South Atlantic schedule. The latter had been maintained by Britannia Airlines during the Gulf campaign. Simultaneously, the Station was busy preparing three VC10s and two TriStars in the VVIP role to fly from Heathrow to Glasgow for the Gulf Memorial Service.

On 15 May a No.216 Squadron TriStar — accompanied by a Harrier and a Jaguar — led a flypast over RAF Cranwell. This was in tribute to Sir Frank Whittle and commemorated the 50th anniversary of the first flight by his jet aircraft. On 23 May No.10 Squadron flew Prince Charles and a group of senior politicians to Delhi for the funeral of Rajiv Ghandi.

On 29 and 30 May an exercise was held to practise procedures for the reception of Russian Inspectors who were coming to the UK under the terms of the Conventional Forces Europe Treaty. On 31 May the Station mounted two flypasts to mark the farewell of Sir Patrick Hine at RAF High Wycombe. The flypast involved a No.101 Squadron VC10K tanker leading a formation of eight Tornados followed by Harriers and Phantoms.

June

Early in June RAF Brize Norton held an in-house Disaster Exercise as part of the Station's return to normal peacetime operations. Late in June, on the 26th, a No.216 Squadron TriStar tanker led a Joint Service flypast over Mansion House. This particular flypast was abridged due to extremely poor weather conditions. Other aircraft were forced to hold off or were stood down, much to the disappointment of crews who had put much effort into practices and rehearsals.

July

On 6 July No.10 Squadron flew Douglas Hurd to Johannesburg. A few days later, the VC10 aircraft was routed back through Ascension Island because mainland staging facilities were not available. During the weekend of 20-21 July RAF Brize Norton gave support to the International Air Tattoo at Fairford. The air space was particularly busy with Brize Radar providing valuable assistance in co-ordinating the air displays. On 31 July a No.216 Squadron TriStar arrived back at the Station, having completed the last flight in support of the Gulf conflict.

August

As if unprepared to relax into mundane operations, RAF Brize Norton became involved, during August 1991, in a most satisfying series of tasks. These comprised the recovery of hostages from the Middle East. The first was John McCarthy, who was brought to RAF Lyneham on 8 August courtesy of No.10 Squadron. On 16 August the new Air Officer Commanding-in-Chief visited the Station and flew with No.216 Squadron.

September

On 7 September RAF Brize Norton raised over £10,000 for the Benevolent Fund and four other Service charities. This was done by an exercise which involved some 40 visiting RAF aircraft from UK and Germany being made available for enthusiasts of aviation photography. On 11 September there was a well-attended JATE visitors' day, and on 12 September the full simulation of a major aircraft crash. The Thames Valley Police, Oxfordshire Fire and Ambulance Services and Local Council authorities joined forces to deal with over 200 'casualties'.

On 23 September the Czech Minister of Defence made an official visit to the UK, and RAF Brize Norton provided facilities for the minister's party, both on arrival and departure. This was closely followed by No.241 OCU bringing home Jackie Mann on 25 September. During September also, No.10 Squadron flew Ministers of State on a tour of the Far East, as well as to Moscow and then on to Harare. On the AAR side, a combined effort by Nos.101 and 216 Squadrons tanked Phantom fast jets to the Falklands between 27 and 30 September.

October

The main feature of October 1991 involved No.10 Squadron mounting VVIP flights for HM the Queen and the Prime Minister to attend the Commonwealth Conference. Between 15 and 23 October, No.101 Squadron took part in an unusual exercise in which they refuelled Mirage aircraft of the Egyptian Air Force. Squadron crews said that flying over the pyramids was less nail biting than refuelling over deserts during the Gulf War.

November

In mid-November Prince Rainier of Monaco arrived and departed in his Falcon 900 aircraft. On 25 November No.101 Squadron flew David Gower on an air-to-air refuelling exercise over the North Sea. However, the most memorable event for November took place on Tuesday the 19th when No.10 Squadron completed its third and final mission to recover hostages from the Middle East — this time Terry Waite. The week continued on a high note with HM the Queen and Prince Philip visiting RAF Brize Norton.

December

The beginning of December 1991 saw No.10 and 216 Squadrons involved in an air-to-air refuelling demonstration for visitors from the Russian Army. The month's work also entailed taking the Prime Minister to and from Maastricht for the EEC Summit Meeting. A third December 1991 item is noteworthy, for this was the month when the OC Operations Wing had an appointment with HM the Queen to be awarded his OBE. The honour recognized the prodigious work carried out by all members of the Wing over what had been a memorable year.

INDEX